Golf Therapy

Golf Therapy

You Are Your Swing

EIGHT CASE STUDIES

By Dr. Bobby Von Hayes
with
Steven Kampmann and Will Aldis

Randt & Company

Randt & Company, Inc.
Ketchum, ID 83340

Library of Congress Catalog Card Number 88-61163
ISBN: 0-942101-04-9

Front cover photo by Christian Gulker
Back cover photo by Lee Tyler

Art consultant, David Kampmann
Illustrations by Evelyn Phillips

Book design and typesetting by Typographics, Ketchum, ID

Distributed to the trade by:
Kampmann & Company, Inc.
New York, NY

Printed in the United States of America
10 9 8 7 6 5 4 3 2 1

I dedicate this book to

BOBBY JONES, CARL JUNG & JOSEPH CAMPBELL

. . . but mostly, I dedicate this book to my Tantric assistants RHIANNON, MORGANA & LAYLA

CONTENTS

Golf Therapy

Preface

Welcome to Golf Therapy. I'm your golf therapist, Doctor Bobby Von Hayes. For years, I've been healing sick golfers, from all over the world, here at the Doctor Bobby Von Hayes Golf Institute in Big Sur, California. But now, thanks to my book, *Golf Therapy: You Are Your Swing,* you don't have to come to the Institute to be cured. You can be helped right in the comfort and privacy of your own home.

Everywhere I go, people ask me, 'Doctor Von Hayes, what exactly is golf therapy?' And I'm intuiting you're asking the same question right now. Golf therapy is simple, really. I believe the only way to become a better golfer is to become a better person, and when I say a better person, I mean a mentally healthy, fully integrated, human being.

You see, as the world's only golf therapist, I have the God-given talent to diagnose what's wrong with a golfer psychologically, just by the way he swings a club. Believe me, I've seen some pretty sick swings in my practice.

In *Golf Therapy: You Are Your Swing,* I present eight case histories, taken from my extensive success file, which demonstrate nine of the most common problems in golf, from hooking and slicing to shanking and yipping. I analyze the psychological roots of these problems and cure them. Trust me, your golfing problem—and its solution—is in this book.

Skeptical? Well, maybe you should be. But before you judge golf therapy, take a look at your own life for a moment. How's your marriage? A little shaky? How's your job? A bit frustrating? How's your sex life? Totally unsatisfying? Now, how's your golf game? Shaky? Frustrating? Unsatisfying? Get the connection? Your life and your game are one and the same.

Still not convinced? Think about this. How many of you golfers out there have taken hours and hours of lessons, read all the golf books, looked at all the instructional videos, and your game hasn't improved at all? Most of you, right? Now, why do you think that is? I'm glad you asked. It's because all those lessons, all those books, and all those videos are trying to convince you that golf is just a game of mechanics and technique. Well, part of it is, but it's also much, much more. Golf is a reflection of who we are. If something is crippling us psychologically, you can bet it's going to show up in our golf swing. Your game doesn't have a chance of improving until you deal with what's ailing you.

Golfers, I'm here for you.

Give me your pain and I'll give you back your game.

INTRODUCTION

Why to Start Playing Golf Again

Every golfer I've ever met has, at one time or another, quit the game. Most have come back. Some, tragically, have not. The most satisfying feeling a golf therapist can have is when he brings someone back to this grand old sport. I did that very thing for the two golfers, Steven Kampmann and Will Aldis, who helped me write this book. Because they're writers, I'll move over and let them tell you their story in their own words. Take it away, fellows.

Thanks, Doctor Von Hayes.

This past spring, at a screening of *Stealing Home,* a

film we wrote and directed, Doctor Bobby Von Hayes asked us if we'd help him write *Golf Therapy: You Are Your Swing.* We told him we'd be honored. You see, if it weren't for Doctor Von Hayes, *Stealing Home* would have never been made.

Four years ago, things weren't exactly jumping for us. Will had recently been fired from a TV show called "People Are Funny," starring Flip Wilson. You may not have seen that show. A lot of people didn't. Will was desperate. In an effort to support his family and supplement his non-existent show business income he decided to apply for a substitute teaching job. This didn't work out so well. During an interview, a high school principal asked Will what he'd been up to lately. Will boasted, "Well, I've done a couple of 'Mork & Mindys,' a Toyota commercial, and a double role in Shelly Duvall's 'Fairy Tale Theater,' where I played a talking tree and Angry Guard #1."

An icy silence fell over the room. "No, Mr. Aldis," the principal replied, "I meant in the field of education."

"Oh," said Will, knowing that his substitute teaching days were over before they'd begun.

So, that night, Will called Steven, his old partner from "The Second City," and asked him if he wanted to meet for a drink. Steven was so depressed he could barely speak. "I can't believe you called. I was just about to call you. I've had the worst day of my life."

You see, that afternoon, Steven had been fired from "Newhart," a TV sit-com about the tiny problems of white people in Vermont. It was okay to lose the show.

That left Plan C. We hit the road, à la *Jack Kerouac and Ken Kesey—write in the car, motels, bars, whatever.*

It wasn't okay to lose all the money he was making on the show. Not only had he just moved his family into an expensive home in the Pacific Palisades, he was doing major construction on that expensive home in the Palisades. He was counting on that money. He needed that money. Without that money he was dead in the water.

Steven was supervising ten construction workers who were putting up the new roof when the producer from the "Newhart" show called to give him the bad news. Steven could barely hear him over the din of buzzsaws and hammerings and other sounds of expensive goings-on.

"Steven, your character will not be returning to the show next year."

"I'm sorry. I can't hear you. There's a lot of construction going on here. Could you repeat that?"

"Your character, Kirk Devane, will not be on the show next year."

"I'm sorry. I really can't hear you. Could you speak louder?"

"YOU'RE FIRED!"

Steven heard that.

"I'M FIRED?!"

Miraculously, all the sounds of construction stopped. You see, Los Angeles is a show business town, and everybody in the construction business knows what it means when an actor is fired from a show. The men packed up their buzzsaws, their hammers, left a large bill, and never came back.

That night, we met at our favorite bar, The Sun Spot, on the Pacific Coast Highway. After three martinis, we convinced ourselves to do what all failed actors in Hollywood do. We decided to write a screenplay. Two martinis later, we came up with a gem of an idea that we were sure no studio in town could possibly turn down. It was called *Cattle Drive:* the story of two funny vaudeville performers in the Old West who win a herd of cattle in a poker game in Dodge City. The catch is they can only collect money on the cattle if they drive the herd two thousand miles to the Chicago stockyards. Needless to say, these two vaudevillians know nothing about cattle drives, so they hire some cowhands who turn out to be even funnier and wackier than they are. The movie is about all the high jinks that happen during the cattle drive. Boy, what an idea!

Now, we just needed a place to write this puppy. We couldn't work at Steven's because his house didn't have a roof. We couldn't work at Will's because his wife was so disappointed in him that the tension was unbearable.

That left Plan C. Hit the road, à la Jack Kerouac and Ken Kesey, free ourselves up—write in the car, motels, bars, whatever—finish it in three days, come back, and sell it in a week. Plan C felt right.

We left the next morning, and the further we drove up the coast, the better the idea got. We were on fire. We had great casting ideas. We'd be the stars. We'd play the funny vaudeville guys. Debbie Reynolds would play the evil lesbian ranch owner, Dan Ackroyd would play the fat, faithful Indian guide, and Bill Murray would be

"Dumpy," the singing cook. It was all coming together.

By the time we reached Big Sur, we had MTV ideas, marketing ideas—everything but a plot. But the hell with the plot. We were hot. Once we found a room and had a few drinks we'd find a plot. Anyone can find a plot.

Unfortunately, not everyone can find a room in Big Sur. Everything was booked. We felt like Joseph and Mary about to give birth to greatness, and there was no room at the Big Sur Inn. We tried Ventanna's. Forget it. We even tried the Tranquility Institute, but Uri, the bearded Israeli guard at the gate, didn't like our vibes and told us to get out. As we were backing out the drive he shouted, "Try the Golf Institute down the road! If you can swing a club, they'll let you in!" So we did.

From this point on, our lives changed forever.

The first thing we noticed as we pulled up the long, tree-lined, pebbled drive was that there were women everywhere. In fact, there were only women. Beautiful women. Already, we liked this place a lot.

As we were checking in, the receptionist seemed to treat Steven with a great deal of deference, as if he were someone special, which we both knew he wasn't.

"You must recognize me from the 'Newhart' show."

"What's that?" she asked.

"It's a TV show."

"I don't watch TV."

"Neither do we," Will said, obviously coming on to her. "We think most TV is garbage. That's why we're screenwriters. Did I mention that we're up here to write a screenplay?"

"No."

"What's your name?" Will said, making his move.

"Rhiannon. I'm one of Doctor Von Hayes' Tantric assistants."

"Excuse me, Rhiannon, but what does Tantric mean?"

"It's from Tantric yoga, which is the yoga of sex. You see, we believe that the act of love is one of the paths to cosmic consciousness."

"Oh, what a wonderful philosophy."

"I'm also a witch."

"Oh, Jesus," Will said, spellbound, "I love witches."

"What's your movie called, and please don't swear."

"*Cattle Drive.*"

"What's it about?" she asked, already bored.

"Well, Rhiannon, it's about two funny vaudeville performers in the Old West—played by Steven and myself—who win a herd of cattle in a poker game in Dodge City and hire some wacky 'Saturday Night Live' types to drive the cattle two thousand miles to the stockyards in Chicago. What do you think?" Will asked, confidently.

"Is that it?" She inquired.

"Yeah."

"Well, there's something wrong with it."

"There is?" Will said cautiously.

"Yes. I mean, is it a comedy, or a tragedy, or what?"

"It's a comedy," Will explained.

"Oh. Well, now I know what's wrong with it."

"What's that?"

"It's not funny."

"It's not?" Will asked, crestfallen.

"No. It strikes me as sad that two men your age would write something as infantile as that."

"Hello," said a soothing voice from behind us.

We turned to see Doctor Bobby Von Hayes, who, except for his silver mane and James Joyce spectacles, looked exactly like Steven. Steven, thinking he was having an out-of-body experience, fainted.

After Doctor Von Hayes had revived Steven, Morgana, another of his Tantric assistants, brought us some fresh-squeezed lemonade and a bouquet of heather.

"There's something about you two gentlemen that intrigues me," Doctor Von Hayes said, speaking exactly like Steven. "I'd like you to stay as my guests tonight and play a round of golf with me in the morning."

"Thank you Doctor Von Hayes, but, actually, we both quit the game years ago," Steven said, sounding exactly like Doctor Von Hayes.

"So?"

"So . . .we stink," Will said.

"Will, here at the Institute, we don't judge our games. We just play them."

"Whew," said Steven. "That's a little heavy."

"Thank you, it is," Doctor Von Hayes said. "So, will you two join me tomorrow morning?"

"Well, I guess we could, but we're a little pressed for time. We're working on a very important screenplay.

What time did you have in mind?'' Will asked.

''Shall we say dawn?''

''You can say dawn, but, of course, I've never seen one,'' Steven joked lamely.

Doctor Von Hayes laughed politely. ''You men are funny.''

''That's our thing. We're comedy writers,'' Will said proudly.

''Not TV writers,'' Steven added quickly. ''Screenwriters. You know. Big movie concept stuff.''

''Well then, I look forward to eighteen holes of laughter tomorrow.''

''When you see our games, you'll *really* be laughing,'' Steven replied.

''Fine, then. See you in the morning.'' Doctor Von Hayes turned and walked away.

That night, we slept like babes in our beds and woke up feeling like we were sixteen.

After being served a breakfast of berries, bran, and goat milk, we met Doctor Von Hayes on the first tee, which overlooked the golf course that cut between the cliffs and canyons of Big Sur.

''This is so beautiful,'' said Steven.

''And peaceful,'' Will whispered.

Doctor Von Hayes closed his eyes and began breathing rhythmically. ''Yes, legend has it that this used to be a sacred Indian healing ground. Of course, I believe that every golf course is a healing ground.'' He opened his eyes. ''I've taken the liberty of providing you each with a set of clubs.''

"These clubs are exactly like the ones I used the day I quit golf," Will said.

"When was that?"

"I was sixteen, playing at the Evanston Community Golf Club. I was two over par on the front nine, which for me was like a miracle, and then I panicked on the back nine and started getting tens and elevens. At the end of the round, I was so defeated that I threw my clubs and my bag into the Evanston Canal. I've never been on a golf course again . . . until now."

"Welcome back, Will. Steven, when did you quit?"

"I quit after my father died."

"Why?"

"Because I . . . uh . . . I don't know. I guess because I figured there was no reason to play anymore."

"You loved him a lot, didn't you?"

"My father was everything to me. We used to play all the time. I remember the last round I played with him. It was a late Sunday afternoon in October and we could see our shadows spreading across the fairways and we could smell leaves burning. I thought we'd go on playing forever. Then he died and I quit."

"Don't be angry at your father for dying. And don't punish yourself for being angry. Just come back to the game and be healed," he said, putting his arms around Steven.

And so, that day, we played a round of golf with Doctor Von Hayes. Will was right. We did stink, but Doctor Von Hayes inspired us. Watching him swing, so effortlessly, made us both fall in love with the game all over again.

Later, sitting on the veranda having lunch, prepared and served by Layla, Doctor Von Hayes' youngest and most beautiful (and naked!) Tantric assistant, Doctor Von Hayes asked us what our movie was about. Surprisingly, we found ourselves embarrassed.

"Well, it's called *Cattle Drive* and it's about . . . "

With every word our idea became smaller and smaller until the Big Sur breeze just blew it away.

"Actually, Doctor Von Hayes, we'd rather not talk about it."

"Listen, I don't know much about the movie business, but can I give you gentlemen some advice?"

"Please."

"Write something that you know. Something that comes from your hearts. Something that has resonance."

"Like what?"

"I don't know. But I do know when you find your swing, you'll find your movie. Experiment. Find a swing that's your own, and you'll find your movie within you. You'll have your true swing when it's smooth and effortless. You'll have your movie when it writes itself. And whenever you lose the thread of your movie, play golf. Work on your swing and your movie will come back to you."

While we took this in, a shadow passed over us. We looked up to see a large elderly man with a graying ponytail. He was wearing a Panama hat, a caftan, and old, washed-out, canvas topsiders.

"Ah, Carlos," said Doctor Von Hayes. "I'd like you

to meet Mr. Kampmann and Mr. Aldis."

Carlos tipped his Panama hat.

"Carlos works at our driving range."

"Where's that?"

"Out there," Doctor Von Hayes said, pointing to the Pacific Ocean. We looked out to see yard marker buoys bobbing in the bay. "Carlos, Mr. Kampmann and Mr. Aldis are screenwriters from Los Angeles."

Carlos spat in the dust and asked, in a thick Mexican accent, "When are you leaving?"

"Today."

"Good," he said, looking right through us. He walked off.

"You'll have to forgive Carlos," Doctor Von Hayes said. "He's had some unfortunate experiences in the entertainment business."

"He looks really familiar."

"It might be best if you forgot Carlos altogether," Doctor Von Hayes advised.

We left that afternoon and headed back to Los Angeles. As we drove down the coast, all we could talk about was golf, movies, and Doctor Von Hayes.

A week later, we were playing a round of golf at the Perfect Liberty Golf Course in Malibu. On the thirteenth tee we both hit perfect drives, smooth, effortless and true. At that instant, just as effortlessly, our movie came to us. We wrote *Stealing Home* in three weeks at the First National Restaurant in the Palisades and sold it five days later.

None of this would have happened without Doctor

Bobby Von Hayes, who brought us back to our game and ourselves. If Golf Therapy can work for us, it can work for you, too. Read this book. Your life and your golf will never be the same.

Back to you, Doctor Von Hayes.

CASE #1:

How to Get Power Back in Your Swing: The Case of Kay Peterson

Are you hitting the ball as far as you think you should? No? The problem may be low self-esteem.

Take the case of Kay Peterson.

Miss Peterson was waiting for me at the driving range. She was lying on a chaise lounge, smoking a non-filtered cigarette, and brushing her ash-blonde, wind-swept hair from her face. I'd be lying if I said she wasn't beautiful.

As I approached, she slowly crossed her legs, revealing a vast expanse of tanned, athletic thigh. Boy, oh, boy.

"Who are you?" she asked, seductively.

"I'm Doctor Von Hayes."

"You are?" she said, coyly.

"You seem surprised."

"I didn't expect someone so young and good-looking."

"Miss Peterson, you don't have to flirt with me."

"I wasn't."

"Sure you were. Just like, when you saw me approaching, you crossed your legs, revealing a vast expanse of tanned athletic thigh. Boy, oh, boy."

"Well, if you didn't like me doing that, why did you say, 'Boy, oh, boy'?"

"I didn't say I didn't like it. But, forgetting all that, Miss Peterson, we're here to talk about your golfing problem, not our obvious mutual attraction. So, what's wrong with your game?"

"I've lost distance in my drives," she said, taking a drag from her cigarette and sensuously exhaling, "I used to be the biggest hitter at my club and now I can't hit worth a damn."

"Please don't smoke and please don't swear, Miss Peterson. Have you had a medical checkup recently?"

"Yes," she said, putting out her cigarette.

"And?"

"I'm fine. In fact, I'm perfect. Don't you think so?"

"Any thyroid or metabolic problems?" I asked, as I gently pressed her thyroid gland, so beautifully encased in her long, swanlike neck.

"No."

"Well, let's see your swing."

Kay, caught up in her anger, hurled her sand wedge at my head, rendering me temporarily unconscious.

She got up, took out her driver, and teed up. She hit a weak shot that barely cleared the cliffs overlooking the sea.

"Hit another one."

She did, weaker than the first. I'd seen enough.

"You have a very beautiful swing, but it has a certain passivity about it. It lacks energy."

"Doctor Von Hayes, you have to help me. I'm desperate. My drives keep getting shorter and shorter, and the club championship is coming up. My club pro has no answers. He's just another weakling trying to come on to me." She was working herself into a state of near-hysteria.

I placed my hand on her forehead.

"Breathe deeply," I said.

When I felt she was calm enough to receive my instruction, I proceeded.

"When was the first time you were aware your drives were becoming shorter?" I asked, imagining a gentle Pacific breeze blowing her skirt over her head.

"It was two years ago, during the club championship."

"What was going on in your life?" I asked.

"Nothing special. I was living with Tommy Python. He's the lead guitarist for the band 'Severe Tire Damage.' You've heard of them, right?"

"No, I'm afraid I haven't."

"You know, now that I think of it, I wasn't going out with Tommy anymore. Actually, we'd just broken up the day before the tournament."

"What happened?"

"I was supposed to meet him at the Roxy, in L.A., for drinks. When I got there, he told me that he was meeting with two female executives from his record label, and could I wait for him at the bar. So I did. I ordered a drink, looked over, and saw Tommy making out with these two women. I mean, right in front of me. And believe me, they didn't look like record executives."

"I know the type. Go on."

"Anyway, all three of them left the bar. I followed them out to the parking lot, where I found Tommy actually having sex with them in the Cadillac Seville that I'd given him for his birthday. I mean, I can take a hint. I figured the relationship was over, so the next day I moved out of my apartment."

"It was your apartment and *you* moved out?

"Yes. That's what I figured he wanted."

"And it was that weekend your drives started getting shorter?"

"Yes."

"Just one more question. Have you had many relationships with men since you left Mr. Python?"

"Too many."

"Just what I figured."

"What do you mean?"

"Well, it's safe to say, Kay . . . may I call you Kay?"

"Please. May I call you Bobby?"

"Not yet.

"Isn't it safe to say, Kay, that you're a poor judge of

men?''

''Yes. That's safe to say.''

She looked down. I gently but professionally lifted her chin.

''And isn't it also true that you flirt with men and use your sex to achieve power over them, because you essentially feel powerless yourself?''

''I don't know. I never thought about that.''

''Isn't that what you were doing to me when you slowly crossed your legs, revealing that vast expanse of tanned, athletic thigh, boy, oh, boy?''

''Maybe. Maybe I was.''

''So that I'd be turned on by you? And all I'd want to do is have sex with you? And not really see who you are as a person? As a human being? And not just as an object of my lust?''

''Yes, yes. God, yes.''

''Don't you understand, Kay, that the moment I saw your swing, I knew everything about you?''

''Doctor Von Hayes, I feel so vulnerable with you.''

''Do you trust me?''

''I'm beginning to. But I still don't understand what all this has to do with my short drives.''

''You will. Take out your sand wedge and walk with me to the Anger Pit.''

As we strolled along the path overlooking the sea, I became aware of certain lustful stirrings within myself. I wasn't ashamed of these feelings. After all, even Dr. Bobby Von Hayes is human. But I'm also a doctor, so I decided to use these sensations to benefit Kay. I remembered a Tantric mantra taught to me by an old golfing monk in Tibet. I chanted as we walked along, bathed in the healing sunlight. Just as we reached the Anger Pit, my baser urges were transformed into pure teaching energy.

I turned to her and said, "What I'm about to do may seem unorthodox."

"Everything about you seems unorthodox."

"Golf therapy *is* unorthodox, but it's effective. Now, Kay, I'd like you to stand in the sand trap—what I call the Anger Pit—and hit these plastic golf balls directly at my face."

"Why?"

"Because I think you're angry at Tommy Python for what he did to you and you've never expressed it."

"But, that was two years ago. Do you really think I'm still angry at him?"

"Did you ever let your anger out?"

"No."

"Well, then why do you think it would ever go away?"

"Gee, I don't know."

"See, Kay, repressed anger is repressed energy. And when you try to repress energy, it weakens you. It weakens your swing. The reason you never expressed your anger is because you have a very low sense of self-esteem. You feel your emotions are worthless. You don't feel you have the right to express them. That's why you flirt with men, to keep them away from what you believe is the worthless you. The weak you. The short-driving you."

"Wow."

"Be gentle, Dr. Bobby," I told myself. "Don't go too fast." I was asking Kay to absorb a lot in a very short time. "Kay, are you ready for your golf therapy?"

"Oh, yes."

"I want you to imagine that I'm Mr. Python, and I want you to start hitting those balls at my face. And, as you do, tell me what you *really* wanted to say to Mr. Python that night in the parking lot."

Kay began hitting shots at me with mounting fervor. Her teeth were clenched and tears of rage streamed down her face.

"Tommy, you son of a bitch! Nobody treats me like this! I am *somebody* and I count! And if I don't count to you, I don't care, because I count to *myself!* And I want you to move out of *my* apartment tonight!"

Kay, caught up in her anger, hurled her sand wedge at my head, rendering me temporarily unconscious.

I came to with my head in her lap. She had torn a sleeve off her blouse and was using it to bandage my wound.

"Are you okay?" she asked.

"Yes," I replied. "Are you?"

She started to weep. "He hurt me so deeply, Doctor Von Hayes. I thought he'd be different."

"We always think they're going to be different, Kay, and they never are. What golf therapy teaches us is not to count on others, but to count on ourselves—that we alone are responsible for what happens to us. If you felt that way whenever you teed off, you'd hit your drives thirty yards farther every time."

"Oh, Doctor Von Hayes. Do you think that's really possible?"

"Kay, some of my Buddhist golfing friends feel that, if we're really in touch with our true Self—our All-Powerful Self—our drives would go on forever and never come down."

We moved to comfort each other and, accidentally, my hand slipped through the sleeveless opening in her blouse, gently cupping her silken bra and feeling the quickened heave of her young breast. I abruptly withdrew my hand and started chanting my Tibetan mantra.

Later, lying on chaise lounges back at the driving range, we sipped herbal Jamaican iced tea and collected ourselves. It had been quite a session.

"Feel better?" I asked. "I mean, *stronger?*"

"Yes," she said, smiling.

"Ready to hit some drives?"

"Sure."

"Good."

Kay went to her golf bag and returned with a one-wood as I teed up an autographed "Bobby Von Hayes" floatable practice ball.

"Let's see if golf therapy works," I said.

Kay addressed the ball and nailed it. It landed well past the 230 yard marker buoy that gently bobbed in the Pacific.

"Wow!"

"Welcome back, slugger."

"Was that for real?"

"Yes. Hit another one. And this time, right before you do, say 'I love me' and see what happens."

She did, and this time the ball sailed well beyond the 250 yard marker buoy.

Kay turned to me. "I'm cured."

"Yes, you are."

"But . . .I thought this would take months."

"As I said to you before, Kay, golf therapy is powerful stuff. I usually see patients only once."

"You mean, I won't be seeing you anymore?"

"You don't need me, Kay. You've got yourself now."

"I only know one way to thank you." Her fingers lovingly caressed my wounded forehead.

"But that would be wrong," I said, furiously chanting my Tibetan mantra.

"If I'm not going to see you again, can I at least kiss you goodbye?"

"Well, I suppose that would be okay."

As the sun set behind us, we kissed. To tell you the truth, I don't remember if the kiss lasted for a moment, or for an hour, or for eternity. But when it ended we knew we both had changed.

"Goodbye, Doctor Von Hayes," she said.

"Call me Bobby."

"Goodbye, Bobby."

"Goodbye, Kay."

As I watched Kay walking down the sloping lawn past the healing center, I thought to myself, "I'll never see this gem again. Not in this life, anyway. Damn the burdens of greatness. Damn my discipline."

And then, that other voice inside me, which sometimes demands to be heard, cried out, "Kay! Kay!"

She turned quickly, the wind revealing a vast expanse of tanned, athletic thigh, boy, oh, boy. I mean, *really* boy, oh, boy. "Life is short, Bobby," the voice inside me insisted. "Be here now. *Carpe diem.*" I ran to Kay and she ran to me and I'd love to share with you what happened next, but that, of course, would break the sacred principle of confidentiality between patient and therapist. In other words, I had the greatest night of my life.

CASE # 2:

How to Lengthen Your Backswing: The Case of Larry McGyver

It was a cool, clear, fall day in Big Sur. Through the French windows in my study, I could feel the crisp apple snap in the air and hear the girlish giggles of my Tantric assistants, who were working in the orchard. It was one of those rare moments of such pure peace and ecstasy that I could no longer contain myself. I stripped and stood buck naked before the open window, letting autumn and ancient childhood memories wash over me. There was a knock at the door and I turned to see, standing before me, Larry McGyver.

"Can I help you?" I asked.

"I'm sorry to disturb you. I must have the wrong room. I was looking for Doctor Von Hayes," he said, staring at me.

"*I'm* Doctor Von Hayes."

"You are? But . . . you're naked.

"You're right. I am," I said, as I put on my gray flannel shorts and my favorite, old, pink, button-down, Brooks Brothers shirt. "And you are . . ."

"I'm Larry McGyver. I just checked into the Institute."

"Great. What's your golfing problem, Larry?"

"Well, I mean, wait a minute. I've got a few questions here before I start discussing my golfing problems. I mean, I walk into this room and you're standing naked in front of the window. I mean, I think that's odd. Why were you naked in the middle of the day?"

"That's a fair question. I was caught up in the beauty of the day and I wanted to be at one with it. My clothes got in the way of that feeling, so I took them off."

"Oh." He paused. "I could never do that."

"That's okay," I said. "Do you have any other questions?"

"Well, sure. I mean, what are your qualifications?"

"Let me show you." I walked him over to the wall where my doctorate degree from the C.G. Jung Institute in Switzerland was hanging. "There," I said. "Satisfied?"

"No. This is a psychiatric degree. I meant your golf qualifications."

"I was on the pro circuit for a year after I got back from Vietnam. Then I quit."

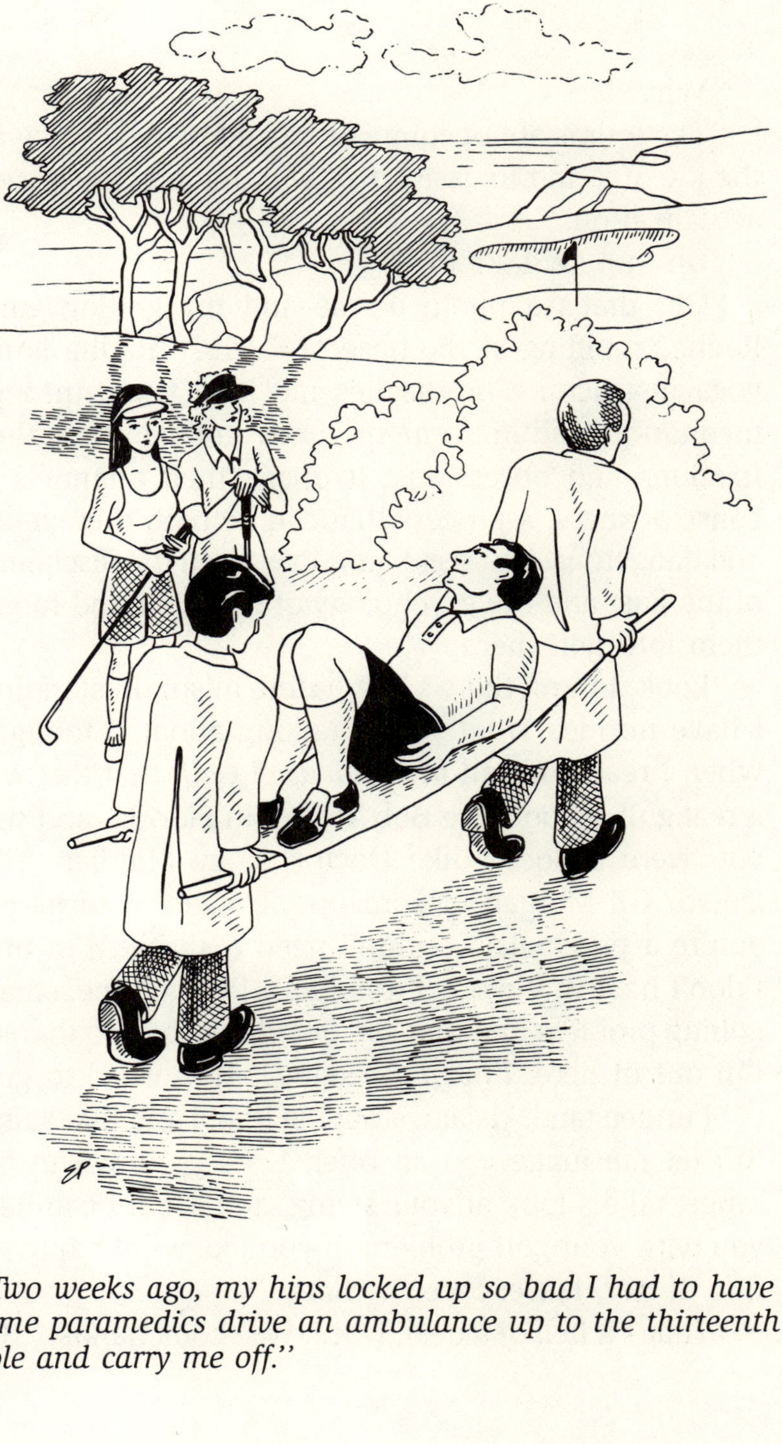

"Two weeks ago, my hips locked up so bad I had to have some paramedics drive an ambulance up to the thirteenth hole and carry me off."

"Why?"

"The tour is about competition and money. I play for the joy of it and to assist people in the process of self-actualization."

"Uh-huh. What's this?"

"Oh, that's a photo of me and my golfing guru, Radha, standing at the base of Everest. Radha is my yoga instructor. She teaches me how yoga, through meditation and movement, frees golfers from their fixations and obsessions. It opens their channels of consciousness, a process that can be both therapeutic and dangerous. You see, Larry, I've taken the disciplines of the East and the psychology of the West and forged them into golf therapy."

"Look, I think there's been some misunderstanding. I have *no* idea what you're talking about. I thought, when I read your ad in *Condensed Golf*, that this was a real golf school, like Bob Toski's in Florida, and that you were a doctor like Doctor Carey Middlekoff or Doctor Gil Morgan or someone. I mean, it turns out you're a psychiatrist. I don't need a shrink. I'm fine. I don't have any mental problems. I've got one, small, golfing problem and that's it. So, thanks but no thanks. I'm out of here. I'm in the wind." He turned to go.

"I understand," I said, stopping him, "and that's fine. But let me make you an offer. Let's go down to my range, take a look at your swing, and see if I can help you with your golf problem. If you like what happens, fine. If not, leave. Free of charge."

"That's a hell of a deal, Doc." We shook hands. "But

any more nudity and I'm history."

On the way to the range, we passed by the orchard.

"Who are those girls?"

"Those are my Tantric assistants."

Larry whistled appreciatively. "I mean, they're so beautiful. And so young."

"If you stick around, you can have dinner with them."

"Oh, I don't know about that. I mean, uh, women scare me. I didn't mean that, Doc, so don't start analyzing me. It's just that I have a lot of dreams about women as big as the Stay-Puff guy in *Ghostbusters* and they're always picking me up and laughing at how small I am. Christ, why am I talking like this? I mean, I just have a small golfing problem. I don't mean small, I mean tiny. I don't mean tiny. I mean I have a *normal* size golfing problem."

"Calm down, Larry," I said, as we arrived at the range. "Now, tell me. What is your normal size golfing problem?"

"When I go to swing, sometimes my hips lock on my backswing. They get stuck. Then I've got just this little, tiny swing and I hit the ball maybe twenty, thirty yards if I'm lucky. My golfing buddies think I'm doing it as a joke, but I'm not. Two weeks ago my hips locked up so bad I had to have some paramedics drive an ambulance up to the thirteenth hole and carry me off."

"Have you seen a physician?"

"Why would I do that? Do you think there's something physically wrong with me?"

"Well, it's not every day that a golfer gets carted away in an ambulance. I think we should take a look at your swing. Maybe that will tell me something."

Larry pulled out a three-wood and teed up.

"Where do I hit?"

"Out into the ocean. Do you see those buoys with the yardage markers?"

There was a long pause while Larry looked.

"This is insane."

"No. This is golf therapy."

"Well, what about the balls?"

"They float. And at the end of the day Carlos, an old fisherman from Carmel, takes his boat out and retrieves them for me."

Larry shrugged and addressed the ball. "And you don't think that's strange, Doctor Von Hayes?"

"No, I don't."

"Okey-dokey. Here we go." Larry began his backswing and, as he went to make his turn, froze into a fixed, locked position.

"There!" he said. "I feel like a piece of granite. I can't move at all!"

"Larry, hand me your club."

"I can't. You're going to have to take it from me."

I tried, but it was impossible. I'd never seen such an extreme case of psycho-sexual paralysis in all my years of golf therapy.

"What's happening to me, Doctor? I feel my throat closing up. I can't breathe! Am I dying? I am dying!"

"You're experiencing an anxiety attack."

"What's that? Is that like a heart attack?!"

"No, Larry," I said, as I placed my hand on his chest.

"Why are you touching me?! Oh, my head feels like it's going to explode."

"Larry. Breathe with me. In. Out. In. Out. In. Out."

It took me thirty minutes to relax him enough to proceed with the therapy. Unfortunately, he still remained paralyzed from the waist down. This was a particularly tough case, because there was so much resistance coming from him.

"I feel better, Doc. If you could give me a shot of Valium or Darvon or something, I'll unlock and be out of your hair in no time at all."

"I don't believe in drug therapy."

"Then, what the hell am I going to do?"

"Please stop swearing and trust me."

"I guess I don't have any choice."

"Larry, how long have you had this problem?"

"Off and on since I was fifteen."

"Why are you coming to see me now?"

"Because it's been getting worse in the last few months."

"What's been going on?"

"Nothing. Except I met this woman I really like."

"What's her name?"

"Daisy Mae. That's not her real name. That's her wrestling name."

"She's a wrestler?"

"Yes. I've always been obsessed with female wrestlers. They're so big. They turn me on and scare me at the same time. I've been following Daisy's career for a couple of years. I'm an accountant, Doctor Von Hayes, and one of my clients is a famous rock singer. I can't mention her name for legal reasons. Anyway, this 'singer' introduced me to Daisy Mae and we really hit it off. But the problem is, now that we've gotten to know each other and gone out a couple of times, she wants to, uh, pin me, if you catch my drift."

"Pin you?"

"Yeah. Put a hammer lock on me. You know, she wants to do the Coco Butt."

"Larry, I'm not familiar with wrestling terms. You're going to have to tell me what you mean."

"SHE WANTS TO HAVE SEX WITH ME!"

"Oh. Well, what's wrong with that?"

"Nothing. It's just out of the question, that's all. Now, I would like to stop talking about this and get back to my golfing problem, because as soon as I began dating Daisy Mae, the locking in this area got worse and worse until, finally, I had the aforementioned humiliating paramedic experience which led me to you. There. Now, why do I have this?"

"Larry, how old are you?"

"I'm twenty-eight."

"And you're a virgin."

"Me? A virgin? Are you out of your mind?"

Larry dropped his club and stared out to sea. Tears welled up in his eyes and then trickled down his cheeks. Embarrassed, he quickly wiped them away. "Yes, I am. This is now officially the worst moment of my life," he said, bending over and picking up his club. "I just unlocked. How did you do that?"

"You did it, Larry."

"But how?"

"By opening up and sharing with me the fact that you're still a virgin. You see, our hip area is our psycho-sexual center. It's very common for golfers' hips to lock, which prevents a long, smooth backswing. In some extreme cases, like yours, the hips become so locked that the backswing is paralyzed and sexual relations become impossible."

"I feel so humiliated and ashamed."

"Larry, if you continue on with me, you'll learn that one of the principles of golf therapy is not to judge yourself. Judgment is its own kind of paralysis. What you need to do, Larry, is to discover who you are and love yourself, not judge yourself. That's what golf therapy's all about. But don't worry, learning not to judge takes time. Right now, I'd like to try something with you, if you still trust me. I'd like you to go up to the Outdoor Healing Center, where my rolfer, Isolde, is waiting for you."

"Rolfer? Isolde?"

"I want you to put yourself totally in her hands. She'll rolfe your lower chakras, in order to break up your psycho-sexual scar tissue."

"Chakras? What the hell are you talking about?"

"Your chakras, Larry, are what yogis believe to be the six centers of consciousness and psychic energy in the body. Your lower chakras control your sexual life.

When these nerve paths are blocked, they need to be rolfed, or manipulated, in order to be opened up. As those pathways are cleared, your sexual self awakens, your hips become unlocked, and your backswing becomes long and full."

"No offense, Doctor Von Hayes, but you sound like a complete nut."

"No offense taken, Larry. On the other hand, you're the one who's going out with a giant wrestler with whom you're afraid to have sex."

"I see your point. What do I do now?"

"Isolde's ready for you. I'll join you in two hours and resume our therapy."

My experience with Larry had drained me. I swung my weighted one-wood two or three times and sensed my swing was out of cosmic harmony. I realized I would have to renew my psychic batteries if I were to be of any use to Larry later on. I repaired to the orchard, where I joined my Tantric assistants, whose laughter, gaiety, and lightness of being soon restored me to my full, natural powers.

As I approached the Outdoor Healing Center, I could hear Larry's screams of agony and ecstasy mingling with the lonely cries of crows.

I found that Isolde had manipulated Larry into a full figure-eight Yoga position, rare even among the most advanced Yoga students. I wasn't surprised. Even though Isolde was only as tall as Linda Hunt, she had hands the size of Kareem Abdul Jabbar with the sensitivity of Vladimir Horowitz.

"I've done everything I can in two hours, Doctor Bobby," said Isolde, wiping the Bali coconut oil from her hands. "If I had him for a week, I think we could make some real progress. He's deeply scarred."

"I know, Isolde. Thanks."

Isolde left, leaving me and Larry alone to resume our therapy.

"Boy, she was terrific," Larry said, untangling himself. She put me in positions I didn't even know existed. I should teach Daisy Mae some of those holds."

"How do you feel in your psycho-sexual center?"

"I'm on fire."

"Good. As I told you before, this area down here is where we generate our sexual energy. Now, take a swing for me. And remember, use your hips to make a complete turn."

His backswing was slow and full.

"Oh, my God!"

"What is it?"

"I'm sorry. I just flashed on my first sexual experience."

"I'm not surprised. When we break up our psycho-sexual scar tissue, it releases past memories that were suppressed. What is the memory?"

"I was fifteen years old. I was at a dance at the Sunnybrook Country Club in Omaha, Nebraska. I didn't belong there. I wasn't even invited. I just snuck in. Then I saw her. Debra Stewart. She was the biggest, blondest, most beautiful girl I'd ever seen, and she was looking at me. We danced to "Chances Are," my head nestled between her breasts. Her corsage kept sticking me in the ear. She suggested we take a walk on the course and, the next thing I know, she'd taken off her party dress and stretched her six foot frame into a sand trap and said, 'Make me a woman, big boy. Make me a woman.'''

"So, what happened?"

"Nothing happened. I tried to get my belt buckle undone, but I couldn't. I finally got it undone and had my pants halfway down when I tripped and landed, face first, into the sand trap. I swallowed a mouthful of sand and started choking, gasping for air. I tried to get up, but I couldn't move. She started laughing uncontrollably. Her laughs turned to shrieks and her head seemed to be getting bigger and bigger, like a crazed balloon. The rest is a blank. That was my first and last sexual encounter."

"Larry, that was a very traumatic experience and I applaud you for being able to share it with me. That was very brave of you."

"I don't feel so great."

"You've been through a lot. What I'd like you to do is spend some time here and continue your sessions with Isolde to break up your psycho-sexual scar tissue. I also suggest that you play golf here every day, and spend as much time as you can with my Tantric assistants, who will reinforce your positive male self-image. You see, that experience you had with the girl at the dance was only one experience, and you're not doomed to repeat it. What happens when we have trauma is that we lock into it, and it paralyses us; i.e., it paralyzes our backswing. One positive experience with one good woman will give you a full backswing for the rest of your life. I guarantee it. When you're done here, I want you to go back to Daisy Mae and take a risk with her."

"Take a risk with her? What does that mean?"

"You know, Larry. Pin her. Do the Coco Butt."

For the first time since I'd met him, Larry laughed.

After two weeks at the Institute, Larry returned to Daisy Mae. A month later, I was in my study, re-reading Michael Murphy's *Golf in the Kingdom* by the fire. The night rain shaped diamonds on my French windows. The phone rang, rousing me from my reverie. It was Larry.

"Hey, Doc. I know it's late, but I had to call you. You wouldn't believe what me and Daisy Mae just did in the sand trap on the thirteenth hole. I pinned her, and my backswing is perfect. I just wanted to say thanks." Larry laughed lustily and hung up.

Golf therapy teaches that golf is life and golf is sex. Larry's call had stirred in me certain primal urges. I stripped and took a long, naked run in the night rain. Later, I stopped in the kitchen for a glass of warm milk and some carrot cake. Then, I visited my Tantric assistants and tucked them all safely into their beds.

CASE # 3:

How to Get In Touch With Your Chipping: The Case of a Former President of the United States

It's common knowledge that women are better chippers than men. Chipping requires a delicate, sensitive feel, the kind of touch that most men lack, because they're not in touch with their feminine side. Carl Jung was the first to describe the two essential selves in each of us; the *anima,* which is the woman in the male; and the *animus,* which is the man in the female. Remember—if you're a man, forty-nine percent of you is female. Recent psychoanalytic golfing research has proven that, if you ignore this sensitive side of your nature, your chipping is going to suffer.

Take the case of a former President of the United States.

I was in the greenhouse working on my pet project, developing a strain of grass that will survive on other planets. Each day I awake and am filled with such sadness and despair when I think of what we are doing to our beautiful Earth. Like many, I fear for the future, and in consequence have made preparations for that fateful day when the chosen must leave for another home. I want to make sure golf goes with us.

I was breaking down the spiral genetics of a blade of Bermuda Blue when I sensed a dark, alien presence entering the grounds. I looked up to see a fleet of black limousines, swirled in dust, coming ominously up the drive. A few minutes later my youngest Tantric, Layla, dressed in . . . well, dressed in nothing, cartwheeled into the greenhouse.

"Doctor, a former President of the United States is here."

"Does he have an appointment?"

"No. Should I tell him to leave?"

"No, I sense his need. Take him to the driving range while I finish up here. Oh, and Layla, perhaps you should put something on."

"Or, perhaps we should all take everything off."

"I hear that, Layla, but imagine this, if you would—the former President of the United States in all his nakedness."

"I'll put something on," she giggled, and cartwheeled out.

Here was the former President of the United States running around in his presidential shorts, thinking he was a woman called Louisa, screaming I'm free! I'm free!

The former President, dressed in a dark suit, was talking to his five Secret Service men as I approached.

"So, fellows, you make money, I make money, and nobody knows the difference. And the beauty of the thing is, even if we do get caught, not a jury in this country would convict us on something like this. Ah, Doctor Von Hayes! There you are. First, let me say, in all candor, that I had nothing to do with all these divots. I didn't make them. They were obviously here before I arrived."

"I know. I did them myself yesterday."

"Good. I just wanted to make that perfectly clear so that we didn't get off on the wrong foot. Secondly, let me apologize for not making an appointment, but, for security reasons, I couldn't." His eyes shifted constantly, like a cornered rat's. Beads of perspiration dotted his upper lip.

"Are you being honest with me?" I asked.

"Probably not," he said. "I was afraid if I called for an appointment, you'd reject me. Or your secretary would."

"Why?"

"Because I always get my secretary to do it when I want to get rid of someone."

"No. I meant why would I reject you?"

"Because of my reputation. You'd be surprised how many people still hate me. Especially you liberal, artsy-fartsy, touchy-feely kind of fellows. No offense, Doctor Von Hayes."

"No offense taken. I'm not here to judge you. I'm

just here to make you a better golfer."

"That's why I'm here. I've got a golfing problem. But I want to make it perfectly clear, it's only a golfing problem."

"Fine. But, before we start, I'm going to have to ask your security men to leave."

"Why?"

"First of all, the sessions are private. And second of all, I don't allow guns at the Institute."

"They're not carrying guns."

"Are you lying?"

"No. Probably. Yes, I am, Doctor Von Hayes."

"Why are you lying again?"

"To test you. I can't respect a man I can fool." He turned to his security men. "Fellows, get lost."

"Now. What's your problem?" I asked.

"Chipping. I can't chip worth a damn. Never been able to. I never get the ball close to the hole. Either I scull it across the green or I flub it and it goes about two inches. See, Doctor, when I get a driver in my hands, I feel powerful. Manly. Presidential. But, when I'm holding a sand wedge, I feel like a girl. There, I've said it. I'm ashamed to admit it, but that's how I feel."

"Feeling girlish is nothing to be ashamed of."

"It is if you're a former President of these United States. I mean, that's a manly job for a manly man, and I'm here to tell you, Doctor Von Hayes, that you're looking at one hell of a manly man."

"I'm sure I am, and please don't swear. Why don't you take off your suit coat and try a few chips?"

"Nope. I always play golf in a full suit."

"Why?"

"It's more presidential."

The former President took out his wedge. On his first chip he sculled the ball off his foot and into the bushes. He clobbered his second chip a hundred and fifty yards out to sea. On his third effort, he buried the ball so deeply into the turf that he had to get on to his hands and knees to pull it out. He had the worst touch of any man I'd ever seen around a green.

"This is humiliating and hardly appropriate for a former commander-in-chief," he said, getting up and brushing off his pants. "You think you can be taken seriously when you chip like that? Look, I'm trying to become an elder statesman and I can't be looking foolish. Take Gerald Ford. He's a national joke because he hits people with golf balls. He'll never be considered an elder statesman. But I will . . . with your help."

"I'll do what I can."

One look at the ex-President's stooped shoulders told me everything. The female side of him, the *anima,* had been repressed, probably from some early childhood trauma. Here was a classic case of a man who was unable to be sensitive and used force, even when force was inappropriate. It was perfectly clear to me that his lack of sensitivity was as much a problem in his life as it was in his chipping. In order to sensitize his chipping touch, I would have to release his *anima.* This was a very dangerous procedure, especially in someone as repressed as the former President. The *anima,* if awakened after a lengthy dormancy, can rage unrestrained through the lower chakras, causing chaos and abnormal behavior.

I warned the ex-President that connecting to his feminine side could be an overwhelming experience, but he waved me off.

"If I can handle Sam Donaldson, I can handle this," he said.

Against my more cautious instincts, I decided to proceed with the therapy, using an Indonesian method of chakra manipulation taught to me by an old British yogi who lives in a lighthouse off the coast of Maine.

"Lie down on your stomach, with your arms spread out in front of you," I instructed him.

I took his sand wedge and placed the club at the base of his spine, near the coccyx. He began screaming. To give him the full brunt of my weight, I balanced myself on top of the club. Within moments his screaming turned into primal female shrieks. His *anima* was released and, as I feared, after so many years of repression, distorted and out of control. He stood up, kicked off his wing-tips, and sensuously peeled off his black ban-lon socks, all the while purring like a cheetah in heat.

"Are you ready for this, Doctor?" he mewed. He slithered out of his slacks, revealing a pair of boxer shorts festooned with the Great Seal of the United States.

I knew I was in deep trouble. "Who are you?" I asked.

"Louisa," he purred coquettishly, whipping off his suit coat and wrapping it around his waist like a dress. "Dance with me," he demanded.

"I don't think that would be appropriate."

"Please. It's been such a long, long time."

"All right." I said, mollifying Louisa.

We began a slow samba as he softly serenaded me with a rendition of Skeeter Davis's "End of the World." He stopped singing and took my face in his hands.

"Oh, it's so good to be free of that cut-off old Quaker. I try to talk to him, Bobby boy, but he never listens. Don't you see? I'm the woman inside him he never lets out, but now I'm free! I'm never going back!"

He bolted toward the greenhouse, in a full-blown psychotic state. Sure, I was concerned about his well-being, but I was also more than a little concerned about my reputation and the reputation of the Institute. After all, here was the former President of the United States running around in his presidential shorts, thinking he was a woman called Louisa, screaming, "I'm free! I'm free!"

I chased him into the greenhouse, startling my Tantric assistants, Layla, Rhiannon, and Morgana, who were drinking cider with the former President's security men.

"Dance with me, my myrmidons!" he sang to his security men. "Take me in your arms and whirl me about in the wind! Let us be light and loving!"

They tried to restrain him, but he broke free, dashed out of the greenhouse, and headed for the golf course. All of us, my assistants, the security men, and myself, gave chase.

For a man his age and with his physical problems, he was incredibly agile and fleet. I finally was able to tackle him around the tenth hole. With the help of my Tantrics, I was able to administer an emergency *anima* normalization procedure taught to me by a Japanese masseuse I lived with one winter in Ketchum, Idaho.

Slowly, Louisa subsided back into the silence of his lower chakras and the President of the United States re-emerged—shaken, but not stirred.

"Where am I?" he asked.

"You're on the tenth hole at my Golf Institute in Big Sur, Mr. President."

"Where are my pants? What have you done to me?"

"Golf therapy is very powerful," I said, as one of the Secret Service men helped the former President into his pants. "I manipulated your *anima* and released the woman inside you. Her name is Louisa."

"Louisa? That's strange."

"Why?"

"Louisa was my great aunt's name. She was a kind, gentle woman. She died when I was a small child. Sometimes I dream of her, but most of the time I don't. Where are my shoes?"

"Right here, Mr. President," said another security man, handing him his wing-tips.

"You've done something to me," he said, while two of his security men tied his shoes. "I don't know what it is. My shoulders feel looser, the tightness is gone, I'm standing more erect. What's going on here?"

"Golf therapy."

A tear came to his eye. "You know, standing out here among all this splendor, I feel a warmth and beauty within me, and a certain sorrow for things I've done. But, then again, maybe I don't."

"Don't deny the woman inside you. That's Louisa coming alive. Recognize her. Be with her. Embrace her. She's your guide. She's your sensitivity. She's your touch around the greens."

"I don't understand what you're talking about. What has this got to do with my chipping?"

"You'll see."

I handed him his wedge and dropped a couple of balls in front of him. He softly lofted a sixty foot chip shot that rolled to within a foot of the pin. He stared at me in disbelief.

"Do it again," I said.

With a swing as smooth as silk, he sank it.

"Well, that's it then. I'm cured. I'm on my way to being an elder statesman. Send me the bill," he said, shaking my hand.

He turned curtly and he and his men walked back to their limousines and drove off. I never saw him again and, of course, he never paid his bill.

Sometime later, I was in the great hall, curled up with my assistants before a roaring fire, watching the Jamie Farr Celebrity Open on TV. To be honest, I wasn't paying much attention until Rhiannon pointed out that the former President was playing. There he was, looking decidedly presidential, and yet his outfit clearly tipped its hat to the woman inside him. He was a study in pink—pink shoes, pink slacks, pink shirt, and even a pink blazer. He stood up to a very difficult sixty-foot chip shot and calmly sank it. He skipped merrily across the green, plucked his ball out of the cup, kissed it, and (I swear) said, "Thanks, Louisa."

CASE # 4:

How to Have Faith in Your Game: The Case of Father O'Gorman

A lot of discouraged weekend golfers come to me complaining they've lost confidence in their game. They honestly think that, by playing once a week, their game will improve. When it doesn't, they lose faith that it ever will. Golf is a demanding game. You get from it what you put into it. If you take your game for granted and never work at it, you'll never improve and you'll never grow as a person. I hate to sound harsh, but it's that simple.

Take the case of Father O'Gorman.

I was giving a lecture on "Tao and the Psychokinetics

of the Golf Swing'' at Northwestern University. After my presentation, I was invited by Doctor Stanley Brown, Dean of the Physics Department, to join him for a round of golf on Easter Sunday at the Indian Pines Country Club in Winnetka.

After an early Easter morning meditation I jogged backwards to the Indian Pines Club. Recently, I've been doing that to relieve the tedium of running and to give myself a fresh perspective on the world.

At the Club, I met Doctor Brown and Father Thomas O'Gorman, Doctor Brown's priest at his church, Our Lady of the Privileged Few. Doctor Brown plays to a ten handicap and Father O'Gorman claimed to be a fifteen, but his game certainly didn't reflect it. He shot a hundred and five on the front nine. At the turn, Doctor Brown kindly suggested a break for lunch, less for nourishment, I suspected, and more to allow Father O'Gorman a chance to recover.

"I'd love to continue the round," Father O'Gorman said stoically, "but I just remembered, I have some church business to attend to. It is Easter Sunday, after all, and I really should be going."

He turned and walked away. In all my years of clinical experience, I'd never seen a more despondent golfer. I quickly ordered my usual jellied consommé, BLT, and a lovely glass of herbal iced tea. Then, I excused myself and followed Father O'Gorman to the parking lot, where I found him, weeping, as he put his clubs into the trunk of his burgundy Coupe de Ville. I put my arm around his shoulder and he wept into my chest.

Faith and a low handicap often go hand in hand.

"Oh, Father Bobby, I'm so lost," he said, his tears staining my polo shirt.

"How long has your game been like this?" I asked.

"Months," he sobbed, "but it's over now. I'm never playing again. When I shanked my drive on the eighth off the ball washer, and it hit Doctor Brown on the forehead, I knew golf and I were finished."

"But, he wasn't injured," I consoled.

"It doesn't matter. When news gets out that my game is no longer in a state of grace, no one will come to confession. I'm ruined."

"Let's walk a while, shall we?"

We left the parking lot and wandered the wooded hills, surrounding the course.

"Doctor Von Hayes, I have something to confess to you. I arranged for this meeting."

"What are you talking about?"

"I convinced Doctor Brown to bring you to Northwestern and I arranged for the three of us to play golf because I had to speak with you."

"Wouldn't it have been easier if you'd just called me at the Institute?"

"Of course."

"Then, why didn't you?"

"Because I'm Catholic."

"I understand. Unburden yourself, Father. Tell me everything."

"Since I was a young novitiate, I've played golf every Sunday, after church. I've always been a fifteen handicap. I could have been a better golfer, but I never practiced. Then, about two months ago, my game went all to hell, if you'll excuse the expression."

"What happened?"

"I guess you might say my game fell victim to the Seven Deadly Sins of golf: Pulling, Duck Hooking, Topping, Slicing, Skying, Shanking, even—I blush to admit it—Hitting Fat. I couldn't account for it. I began to lose faith that I'd ever get better. The other priests said it was normal to doubt your abilities on the course from time to time. Still, I was troubled and my game kept getting worse.

"So, I went to the Archbishop of Chicago, who told me to go see the Holy Father, in Rome. He confided in me that the Pope, like myself, had also lost faith in his game as a young man.

"So, I made the pilgrimage to the Vatican, where His Holiness received me and said, 'Do what I did in my moment of spiritual golfing crisis.'

" 'And what was that, Your Eminence?'

" 'I went to see Doctor Bobby Von Hayes.'

" 'Doctor Von Hayes?' I asked.

" 'Yes, my son. He's the world's only golf therapist and a man of true vision.' "

"His Eminence is too kind," I said to Father O'Gorman.

"At any rate, the Holy Father told me to see you. So what was I going to say? No?"

"And here we are," I said.

We stopped on a hill that overlooked the course and the placid shores of Lake Michigan.

"Tell me about your work at the parish."

"Our Lady of the Privileged Few has the wealthiest parishioners, per capita, of any diocese in the Midwest. My flock reads like a 'Who's Who' of business and government. It's a very impressive establishment, Doctor Von Hayes."

"I'm sure it is. And yet, I don't hear any joy in your voice when you describe it to me. What exactly do you do there?"

"I tend to my flock. Well, actually, they tend to themselves pretty well. They come to confession, I quickly exonerate them and send them on their wealthy way. Then, of course, there are the benefits and social functions, where I stand around and listen to their sacrilegious golfing jokes and try not to get too drunk." He paused for a moment.

"So, I take it you have a lot of time for prayer?"

"I wish you hadn't asked that. You see, I've stopped praying. I'm too busy being busy. I've stopped speaking with Him. I don't even know if He's there anymore. My God, I think I'm losing my faith."

"It shows in your swing."

"It does?"

"Of course. Your swing has no consistency. It changes from stroke to stroke, which means you have no center, no foundation; which means you've lost your faith. That's why you feel the Devil's invaded your game."

He let this sink in for a moment. "You know, I always thought I wanted to be a priest at an exclusive parish on the North Shore. And now that I am, I couldn't be farther away from my God."

"Or from your game."

"What exactly are you saying, Doctor?"

"I'm saying that you've taken God for granted, just as you've taken golf for granted. You don't practice, and you don't pray. God requires more than just faith, he requires works. So does golf."

"But, there's nothing to pray for at Our Lady of the Privileged Few. My parishioners have everything already. What should I pray for? More prosperity for them, when ghetto children six miles away are starving in the streets?"

We walked down the hill to the parking lot.

"Maybe I shouldn't stay at my parish. I'm so confused, I don't know what to do."

"Ask God," I said.

"How?"

"Pray."

"When?"

"Now."

"You mean, pray right here, in the parking lot?"

"Why not?"

"What will people think?"

"They'll think, 'There's a priest, praying.' Sounds pretty normal to me."

"I don't think I can do it. Not here."

"Then, I'll pray with you." I knelt down on the gravel and motioned for him to join me.

He looked around to make sure that no one was watching, then reluctantly knelt down beside me.

"What are we praying for?" he asked.

"A sign from God. If you have faith, one will come. We'll stay here until it does."

"Okay," he shrugged. "The Pope did say your methods were unorthodox."

We prayed vigorously for an hour or so, then I turned to him. "Are you getting anything at all?"

"Not yet."

"How are you doing?" I asked.

"My knees are killing me. Can't we move over there to the grass?"

"We made a commitment to stay right here. Have faith. He'll send us a sign. He's just testing us."

A horn blared behind us. We turned to see a Mercedes-Benz sedan filled with angry Republicans.

"What are you two doing?" they shouted.

"We're praying. Could you please go around us?"

"Praying in the parking lot? What are you, maniacs? Get out of the way!"

"We can't. Father O'Gorman here is waiting for a sign from God."

"Oh, Jesus Christ!" one of the Republicans bellowed.

"Please don't swear," I requested.

"Uh-huh. You're going to hear about this, Father." The car roared past, spraying us with gravel.

"I really wish we weren't doing this," Father O'Gorman said. "Those gentlemen are members of my parish."

Another hour passed without a sign. Then, a security guard pulled up in a golf cart. Was this our sign, I wondered?

"I've received several complaints about you gentlemen. I'm going to have to ask you to leave."

"I'm afraid that's not possible. You see, Father O'Gorman is waiting for a sign from God."

"Why don't you guys go have another drink somewhere else?"

"We haven't been drinking," I said.

"Yeah, right. How'd you get in here?"

"I'm a guest of Doctor Brown's," Father O'Gorman said, taking a deep breath and crossing himself.

"Uh-huh. I'll be back," said the security guard. He peeled out in his golf cart, spraying gravel all over us.

"I think God has completely forgotten about me. And I deserve it. You're right. I don't practice golf, and my game has fallen apart. I don't pray to God, and he's abandoned me."

"Be patient. The Lord works in mysterious ways."

Just then, the security guard returned with Doctor Brown.

"What's going on here?" Doctor Brown demanded. "Doctor Von Hayes, I've been waiting in the club house for two hours for you to join me for lunch and now I hear, Father O'Gorman, that you're praying and blocking traffic and disturbing the peace."

"Father O'Gorman is waiting for—"

"Please, Doctor Von Hayes," said the priest, "don't try to explain."

"Father O'Gorman," Doctor Brown said sternly, "this behavior is totally unacceptable, especially coming from a priest at Our Lady of the Privileged Few. I'm going to call an emergency board meeting for tomorrow evening and recommend that we find you a new parish."

"I understand," said Father O'Gorman. "And I'm sorry I hit you on the head at the eighth tee."

Doctor Brown and the security guard wheeled away, spraying us with gravel.

"This is all my fault, Father O'Gorman. I'm truly sorry."

"Don't be sorry, Doctor Von Hayes," he said, beaming, "the Lord has just given me a sign!"

We left the Indian Pines Country Club and went to a public golf range to practice, something Father O'Gorman hadn't done in a long time. I left him on the second tier to be alone with his swing and his thoughts, while I worked on a shot I'd been inventing—a wedge spin drop shot that spirals in diminishing circles to the hole.

A few buckets later I rejoined Father O'Gorman on the second tier. He was glistening with sweat and smiling beatifically.

"My swing's coming back to me, Doctor. It feels natural again. And after my second bucket of balls, I actually spoke with Him."

"I hope your talk was fruitful."

"Very. After we reacquainted ourselves with one another, we decided it was a good thing for me to leave Our Lady of the Privileged Few."

"Good. So, what are you going to do?"

"We haven't decided. We're just going to keep talking. And keep practicing."

Father O'Gorman and I shook hands. He blessed me and we went our separate ways.

Four months later, I was back at the Institute, playing Jerry Lee Lewis's "Great Balls of Fire" on the piano, when Rhiannon flipped in, left a telegram on the piano, and flipped out.

It was from Father O'Gorman, and I'd love to share it with you.

Dear Doctor Von Hayes,

I'm writing you from Saint Anne's parish on the South Side of Chicago. We are the poorest parish in the city, but I've never felt more fulfilled. They need me here.

Oh, by the way, I don't play golf at Indian Hills anymore. The kids and I use a little nine-hole municipal course that's more brown than green, but my game's never been better. Of course, when you practice every day and pray every night, good things just seem to happen.

Pax Vobiscum,

Father Tom

CASE # 5:

How to Play the Sand Shot: The Case of Sandy Bates

One of the most common golf problems that patients come to me with is sand trap phobia. You'd be amazed at what golfers will do to avoid this hazard.

Take the case of Sandy Bates.

Carlos and I were out in his boat, the "Bounty," observing the sexual habits of the grey whales who swim by the Institute every March on their way to Baja. Carlos has an uncanny knack of mimicry and is able to imitate the mating calls of these behemoths of the deep. His favorite, Jean-Baptiste, was being particularly flirtatious with the cows on this gentle spring afternoon.

Suddenly, the rhythmic slapping of flukes on water was drowned out by the mechanical whirring of helicopter blades directly above us. A frantic little fellow in a three-piece suit screamed down at me.

"ARE YOU DOCTOR VON HAYES?"

"YES, I AM!"

"I NEED TO SEE YOU, NOW!"

Bemused, Carlos and I watched this frenzied gentleman lower himself down a rope-ladder, a huge lizard-skin golf bag slung over his shoulder. He jumped aboard the "Bounty" and waved the helicopter off.

"Hi, Doctor. I'm Richard Bates, but everybody calls me Sandy."

"You seem to be in a bit of a rush, Sandy."

"That's the street where I live, babe. Time is money. Money is time. So, let's cut to the chase, Doctor. I've got a problem. A big golfing problem. Here's the deal. I've got a microjet waiting for me in 'Frisco to take me to Hong Kong, where I've got a match with three Oriental dudes from the largest banking cartel in the Far East. Now, my jet takes off in an hour, which leaves me half an hour with you. Here's a check for ten thousand dollars. Fix me."

"I'm not in the fixing business, Sandy. I'm in the healing business."

"Heal me, schmeal me. Just do it!"

"I'll try. What's your problem?"

"Sand traps."

"You don't know how to get out of them?"

"No. I never get in them."

"DOCTOR VON HAYES?! I NEED TO SEE YOU! NOW!"

"That's wonderful."

"No, it isn't. It's awful. I'll do anything to avoid them. I used to be a five handicapper. Now I'm a thirteen. You know why? If there's a trap in front of me, I'll chip around it. I'll take a bogie instead of going for the birdie. It's killing my game, and my game, Doctor Von Hayes, is big business. You see, I've got a lot of action going in the Far East, and when those little fellows come over here they want to play the great American courses. I'm a member of Spruce Valley, perhaps the greatest course in the world. Have you ever played there, Doctor Von Hayes?"

"I haven't had the pleasure."

"I'll take you there, sometime. Anyway, I get these guys on the golf course and when they see me chipping around sand traps do you know what they smell? They smell fear. And when they smell fear, the deal is gone. And the deal is my blood, Doc. I haven't made a deal in so long I can't even think about it. I'm drying up," he said, pressing his palms against his temples. "I'm panicking."

"You seem anxious."

"Of course I'm anxious. I have heart palpitations. I have an ulcer. I'm falling apart. What are those?" he said, pointing out to sea.

"Whales," Carlos said, without looking at him.

"What are they doing?"

"Making babies," Carlos grunted.

"Lucky them. Come on Doc, I've only got twenty-four minutes left. Let's go, let's go, let's go!"

There was no time to get back to the Institute and work out Sandy's problem in the Anger Pit. Fortunately, we were only moments from the beach.

"Have you always had problems with sand traps?" I asked, as Carlos rowed the "Bounty" to shore.

"Are you kidding? I'm a member of Spruce Valley, it's all sand there. I love sand. That's why my friends call me Sandy. My real name's Richard. Did I tell you that already?"

"Yes."

"I don't remember telling you that. I'm losing my memory, too. This sand trap problem is giving me Alzheimer's disease."

"Relax. Breathe deeply," I advised.

He breathed in once. "It's not working. Now what? We've got twenty-two minutes. Let's move it."

"Okay. When did you start experiencing problems with sand traps?"

"I don't remember. See. Alzheimer's."

"Please try."

"I can't," he insisted.

"Concentrate."

"Forget it," he said, defeated.

"Tell him or I'll kill you!" Carlos bellowed, as he hoisted Sandy up by his lapels.

"All right, all right! I'll try," Sandy said. Carlos put him down. Sandy held his head in his hands, trying to concentrate. In the distance, Jean-Baptiste breached, waving goodbye with his flukes.

"I remember!" Sandy said. "It was a year and a half

ago. I was playing with two honchos from Honda. The stakes were high. You see, you play American businessmen and you stroke them. You lose so you can get the account. It's a whole other ball of wax with those Oriental cats. If you beat them, they respect you, and they'll do business with you. If you lose, you're out. Sayonara."

"So, what happened?" I asked.

"Do I have to talk about this? It's painful."

"Do you want to get better?"

"Yes."

"Then let's deal with it. What happened?"

"Okay. Like I said, I was playing at Spruce Valley with these two guys from Honda. I was one up going to the tenth hole, which is a par three that isn't particularly difficult, except for one trap that we affectionately call the 'Devil's Armpit.' I hit my eight-iron a little fat and dumped it dead center in the D.A. I couldn't believe it. The last thing I remember was walking down the steps into the trap. That's it, Doc. The rest is a blank. Next thing I know I'm looking across the desk at my C.E.O., who tells me Honda is history. That's the first account I ever lost, and I've been losing accounts and avoiding sand traps ever since."

Carlos jumped out of the boat and pulled us onto the beach. I got out and began digging in the sand. "What are you doing?" asked Sandy, looking at his watch.

"I'm digging a model of the Devil's Armpit."

"Why are you doing that?"

"Because you're getting in it."

"No way."

"Listen, Sandy. Until you re-experience what you repressed that day at Spruce Valley, you'll always have a fear of sand traps. And as long as you're carrying that fear around with you, your game will never improve. And apparently, if your game doesn't improve, your business won't either. It's that simple."

"I'm not paying you ten thousand dollars to dig in the sand, Doc."

"Dig!" Carlos growled. Sandy dug.

Five minutes later we had a passable replica of the Devil's Armpit, eight feet wide and five feet deep.

"What did you hit out of the trap that day?"

Beads of sweat were forming on Sandy's brow. "I can't remember."

"You've got to."

"My instincts told me to use my sand wedge, but I panicked and used my pitching wedge instead. I thought I could get more height with it, but I was wrong."

"Go with your instincts now. Grab your sand wedge."

He did.

"Now get in the trap."

"I'm frightened."

"Get in, or I'll throw you in!" Carlos barked.

"I get the feeling Carlos doesn't like me."

"I don't."

"Why not? I haven't done anything to you."

"Yeah, you did. You ruined my day with the whales. And, besides, you're a wimp. You're afraid of sand traps.

Give me a break. Be a man."

"Haven't I seen you somewhere before, Carlos?" Sandy asked.

"No. Now get in or I'll break your legs!" Carlos roared. Sandy jumped into the 'Armpit.' As you can tell, Carlos has a way of getting results.

"Now what do I do?" Sandy asked.

I took a ball out and threw it to him. "Pretend this oar over here is the pin. Now, hit out. But, before you do, tell me where the two businessmen were standing."

"They were behind me."

"And what were they doing while you were in the trap?"

"What difference does it make?"

"Sandy, pay attention. We're going to perform an intense psycho-drama here. Carlos and I are going to play the Japanese businessmen. You're going to re-live a very painful experience. It's going to be very unpleasant but you will survive it. Trust me."

"Okay."

"Now, what were the Japanese businessmen doing while you were trying to get out of the D.A.?"

"Well, in the beginning they were very polite. Then they became less and less inscrutable and began whispering rapidly, saying terrible things about me, I'm sure."

"Like this?" Carlos and I began whispering.

"Yes, just like that."

"Now, start hitting."

Sandy flailed away in the trap, sending sand

everywhere. He began groaning, and soon he was yelling, "I can't get out. I can't get out. Stop whispering about me! I can't get out! I can't get out!"

"Then, what happened?" I shouted to the desperate Sandy.

"They started laughing so hard they fell down."

"Like this?" Carlos and I tumbled to the ground, laughing.

"No! More like insulting hyenas! Yes! That's it! That's it, you bastards!"

"Keep hitting!"

"Why?! I'm never going to get out of here! With every swing I'm digging my grave! I'm trapped! I'm trapped in here! I'm trapped in the Devil's Armpit!! I'm dying! I'm dying in here! Help me! Help me! Help me!"

He had gone over the psychic red-line. We leapt into the pit and pulled him out. This type of psycho-drama is extremely powerful. Sandy was convinced we were the Japanese businessmen. He grabbed Carlos around the throat.

"You happy now, you sons-of-bitches?! You happy to see a red-blooded American take a five hundred and fifty-seven on a hole?! You can take your Hondas and your Sonys and your Mitsubishis and get out of the good old U.S. of A.! Get out! Get out!"

I had to slap Sandy back into reality. "Let go of Carlos, Sandy! It's me, Doctor Von Hayes! You're in Big Sur. You're not in the Devil's Armpit. And you're okay. You're okay. Breathe deeply. That's right. Deeply."

Sandy's eyes lost their glaze and focused on me. "Oh,

I'm so ashamed," he cried. "Now I remember. I attacked those nice little fellows and chased them all the way back to their Hondas in the parking lot. Oh, God. What have I done?"

"It's over, Sandy. It's all over."

Sandy sobbed in Carlos's arms. "Do you know why my mother called me Sandy, Carlos? Because no one could ever get out of sand traps like her little boy Sandy. But, you want to know the truth, Carlos, old friend? I never knew what I was doing, it was just something I could do. It was all just luck, and now I'm not lucky anymore!" he screamed into Carlos's face. "It's over! My life is over!"

Carlos slapped him. "Calm down and stop blubbering. You're going to be all right. Doctor Von Hayes will take care of your stupid little problem."

"Thanks, Carlos," Sandy said, sweetly. "You're very sensitive."

"Sandy, there's something very important you must realize," I said. "The reason you played well out of sand traps had nothing to do with luck. You were born a natural sand trap player. Trust that about yourself. One bad experience doesn't negate who you really are. Accept that."

Just then, we heard the whirring blades of Sandy's helicopter approaching.

"There's a lot more to teach you, Sandy, but I'm afraid our session is just about up. There is, however, enough time left to show you a special interlocking overgrip for sand traps taught to me by Ian McLyle, my old instructor at St. Andrews."

We jumped down into the pit and I showed him the grip. "Along with this, Sandy, the key is to make an inside upright move with your backswing with a ninety-one degree angle to your right knee. Then, just make sure you follow through with a little hand action. Like this."

My ball popped out of the trap and landed an inch away from the oar.

"That's great. You mean like this?" Sandy did it and his ball flew out of the pit, landing near mine.

"Do it again."

He did.

"And again."

He did.

"I'm cured."

"Not quite, Sandy. Anyone can learn technique. There are a thousand teachers who can teach it, and yet most players never break a hundred. Golf is a game of trust—trust in yourself. Now, when you land in a sand trap, don't think of golf's hazards or life's hazards as opportunities for failure. Think of them as opportunities for success."

The helicopter now hovered above us and the rope-ladder dropped. "Go to Hong Kong. And remember, Sandy, you're a samurai. Here's your sword." I handed him his sand wedge.

"Thank you, Doctor Von Hayes. You know, I feel like I'm just scratching the surface here. There's more to this game than just sand traps, isn't there?"

"That's right, Sandy, and there's more to life than just business. Come back and see us some time."

"I will." He confidently jumped out of the sand pit, picked up his golf bag, and climbed up the rope-ladder. He stopped and looked down at Carlos.

"Hey, Carlos!"

"Yeah?"

"I know who you really are. But I won't tell anybody. I promise."

"You're okay, Sandy," Carlos called back.

"So are you, Carlos."

We watched as Sandy and his helicopter disappeared over the Monterey Peninsula. We got in our boat and rowed back into the bay. While I read from the collected poems of Dylan Thomas, Carlos stood in the bow and called out to his beloved friends of the deep, "Waah-ooh-waah-ooh, waah-ooh-waah-ooh."

CASE # 6:

How to Get the Yips Out of Your Putts: The Case of Stuffy McWorter

Putting is the most individual part of your game, reflecting what Carl Jung calls the ''individuation process.'' What this means is that there are no general rules about putting technique. What works for one player may not work for another. Sam Snead, for example, uses a croquet style of putting, while Bernhard Langer putts cross-handed. Personally, I only putt with my left hand, while my right hand is casually placed in my pants pocket. You probably think that's odd, but it works for me. The point is, you have to find the right technique for yourself, and you can't do that unless you know who you are.

Take the case of William McWorter IV.

I was out on the putting green, awaiting my lesson with Mr. McWorter. I was nursing a cold and feeling a little out of sorts. Obviously, my energies were diffused and my chakras were out of alignment. So I hung by my knees from a low-hanging limb of a cypress tree. I was relaxing into an alpha state when I heard footsteps. I opened my eyes to see, before me, a pair of loud red pants with little green pheasants on them.

"Doctor Von Hayes?" said the pants.

"Yes," I replied, looking up into a pair of patrician nostrils.

"I'm William McWorter IV," he said, "but my friends call me Stuffy."

I flipped off the tree, landing squarely in front of him.

"Yipes!" Stuffy said, breaking wind, "that scared me."

"I'm sorry, Scruffy."

"It's Stuffy, actually."

"Stuffy? What kind of name is Stuffy?" I asked this short, unformed, inner tube of a fellow.

"Well, actually it's a nickname my father gave me."

"Why?"

"Golly day. It's been ages since I've thought about why he called me that. Has the therapy already begun without me knowing it, Doctor Von Hayes?"

"I don't know. Maybe. When did your father first call you Stuffy?"

"Well, uh, I believe it was when I was, uh, five," he

"Hello, putter," Stuffy said, tentatively.

said, his left eyelid twitching. "It was during the annual McWorter Thanksgiving dinner when the entire clan was gathered: my mother; my big brother, Buck; the twins, Katherine and Cecelia; and, of course, the Senator."

"The Senator?"

"My father. He doesn't like to be called Dad. He insists we all call him 'The Senator.' It was at that very meal I called him Dad by mistake and he said, 'I've told you never to call me Dad. And just for doing that, William, we're all going to call you Stuffy from now on for stuffing all that stuffing into your chubby little cheeks, you tubby little turkey.' I believe those were his exact words."

"My God. What did you say?"

"Well, I believe I was so stunned that I started stuttering uncontrollably and everybody laughed at me."

"You don't have to call me 'The Therapist.' You can call me Bobby, and I'll call you Bill. Is that all right?"

"Great."

"What's your golf problem, Bill?"

"Well, Bobby. I should be a ten handicapper, except I average over forty putts a round."

"Forty?"

"Yeah, forty. Does that mean I'm insane?"

"No, it doesn't. It's just that forty putts is a lot."

"Yeah, and lately it's getting worse and worse, Bobby. I'm yipping like a lunatic."

"Well, let's take a look." I threw a couple of balls down on the practice green.

He brought his bag over and pulled out a 1941 Tommy Armour putter.

"That's a beauty."

"Thanks. It's the Senator's."

"He gave it to you?"

"Yeah, well, he kind of insists I play with it—that is, if I want to receive my trust fund. I get it on my fortieth birthday. You know how most fellows get their trust funds when they're twenty-one? Well, not me. The Senator said, 'A stupid little Stuffy like you wouldn't know what to do with all that money until he was a fat forty little fool.' I believe those were his exact words. Perhaps I'm revealing too much."

"Usually we don't reveal enough," I observed.

"Can I putt now?" he said, quickly.

"Sure. Let's try some two-footers."

He yipped all of them. He was totally incapable of a smooth, directed stroke.

"See, Bobby? I can't stop the yips."

"I've never seen a stance like that. You're very rigid."

"It's the way the Senator putts. He's a great putter."

"I'm sure he is. But you know what, Bill? I'd like you to try another putter. Just for fun."

"Oh, I couldn't do that. I've always used this one."

"What's that putter in your bag?"

"Oh, that's nothing," he said, pulling out an old cut-off, hickory-shafted putter. "That's just my old putter, from when I was a boy. I found it up in my parents' attic and I was thinking of giving it to my son for his eighth birthday."

"I had one like this. It has great feel," I said, sinking a sixty-footer. "I want you to try something. Do you trust me?"

"Sure. I guess so."

"I want you to talk to your putter, as if it's an old friend you haven't seen in a long time. Then, I want you to talk to you as if you were the putter."

"Sounds pretty weird, Doctor."

"It's not. It's a very common gestalt technique. Go ahead."

"Hello, putter," he said, tentatively. "You mean like that, Bobby?"

"Yes. Now be the putter."

"But . . . I don't know what a putter would say."

"It's been a long time since it's seen you. What do you think it would say?"

"Long time, no see. What have you been up to?" said the putter.

"Not much," Bill replied. "After I put you in the closet I finished grade school and then high school and went to college and got married and . . . had a son. How about you? What have you been doing?"

"Well, nothing. I've been in the closet, where you abandoned me, thank you very much."

"I didn't abandon you."

"Sure, you did. The Senator told you it was time to put childish things behind you, so you put me in the closet, even though I'd never let you down. Don't you remember the time we won the Junior Club Championship by sinking that twenty-foot putt on the eighteenth? Or, have you forgotten about that?"

"I haven't forgotten."

"Then, you abandoned me. That really hurt. By the way, why are you wearing those stupid red pants with birds all over them? Don't tell me. The Senator gave them to you for your birthday. Haven't you gained a lot of weight? You don't even look like you anymore. Who are you, anyway?"

"I don't know."

"I do," said the putter. "The Senator's right. You're Stuffy McWorter."

"No, I'm not!"

"Then, who are you?"

"I don't know. Doctor Von Hayes, who am I?"

"I can't tell you that, Bill, but I can tell you a lot of golfers don't know who they are, either. That's why they're always trying to putt like someone else, and it never works. The more they copy, the more they yip. You see, when it comes time to make a putt under pressure, they're so out of touch with their real self and their own, individual putting technique, they can't help but yip."

"Yipes, you're right. Every time I putt, I always try to copy the Senator."

"You need to reacquaint yourself with an old friend, William," I said, handing him his boyhood putter.

He took it. "I feel really badly that I abandoned it."

"Bill. The past is the past. Now is now. Let's sink some putts."

Bill assumed the Senator's rigid golfing stance.

"This putter doesn't reach the ground."

"That's because you're putting like your father and not your true self, the one you deserted when you were a child. Get comfortable with your putter. Be one with it."

Bill crouched over and smoothly sank a five-footer, then a ten-footer, then a twenty-footer, and, finally, a sixty-footer.

"I'm cured," he said, kissing the putter's blade.

"Of course you are. That's the putter you were meant to play with, and that's your real self putting."

"You're right, Doc. I'll never use another putter again."

"Then, you'll use it the next time you play the Senator?"

"Oh, well, uh, I don't know about that. I think it might be smarter to use his putter and his stance. Just when I play him. I'll use my old putter everywhere else."

"Then I think you ought to just put that putter back in your closet, because you haven't learned anything here."

"Well, what am I meant to say to him when he sees I'm not using his putter?"

"What would your old putter say to him?"

"Oh, that's easy. It'd say, 'From now on, I'm his real putter. And if you don't like it, you can take your 1941 Tommy Armour and stuff it. And speaking of stuffing, the name is William from now on, not Stuffy. Okay, *Dad?*'"

"Well, I think your putter said it all, Bill. Don't you?"

Bill paused for a moment, looking down. "That's easy

for my putter to say. I don't know if I can say it. Anyway, thanks for the lesson, Doc. I've got to get going."

As I watched his plump little figure waddle away, I really doubted he would have the courage to stand up to his father.

That Sunday evening, I was in my library having a hot whiskey toddy while Rhiannon massaged my feet and Morgana read to me from Turgenev's *Fathers and Sons.* The phone rang.

"Hey, Bobby, it's me, Bill. Guess what? I played Spyglass today with my father. I beat the old Senator on the eighteenth when I sank a twenty-footer with my old putter. And you know what the Senator did, Doctor Von Hayes? He put his arm around me and said, 'Nice putt, William.' Yippee!"

CASE # 7:

How to Play with Your Mate, or Who's Afraid of a Little Golf: The Case of George and Martha Meade

Why is it that men and women don't play golf together? There's the PGA tour and then there's the LPGA tour. Tuesdays and Fridays at the club are reserved for the women and the rest belong to the men. Men say that women play too slowly and women say that men are too competitive. Men and women can't get it together on the golf course. That should come as no surprise. They can't get it together in life. Look at the divorce rate in this country. I believe that if men and women could learn to play golf together, the quality of their relationships off the course would improve as well.

Take the case of George and Martha Meade.

I was in our Pro Shop, talking to Don Levy, my golf therapy intern from the University of California at Santa Cruz.

"Who am I seeing today, Don?"

"A married couple. George and Martha Meade."

"What's their background?"

"Well, he's an English professor at Albey College and she's the daughter of the Dean."

"What's their problem?"

"They were just put on probation at their country club for fighting on the course."

"We've seen that problem before, haven't we, Don?"

"We sure have, Doctor Von Hayes. Listen, speaking of men/women problems, I wonder, if you have a minute, if I could discuss a problem I'm having."

"Sure, Don."

"Doctor, I don't want to sound like a swine, but I just want to have sex with your assistants all the time. It's all I can think about. Take Rhiannon, for example, with her beautiful breasts straining against her pink Bobby Von Hayes polo shirt and, I'm convinced, yearning to be set free. Or Morgana, with her wild red mane that I'd like to bury my face in for the rest of my life. And then, there's Layla, who runs around naked all the time. What am I meant to do? Pretend I don't see her? I'm a young man on fire."

"Don, if my assistants are troubling you so deeply, perhaps you should leave the Institute."

"Oh, no! Don't make me leave! Besides, I can't leave.

"I don't think I can save her."

I'd lose all my extra credit at the University."

"Then, you're going to have to learn to harness your sexual energy and use it to improve your golf swing. By the way, let me see your swing."

Don picked up a club and took a swing.

"Oh, I see what's going on. Your backswing is way too fast, which tells me that you want to hurry up and get your swing over with. You treat the golf ball as an object to be dispensed with as quickly as possible. You're the same way with women. You treat them as sexual objects. They're to be had for your pleasure and then abandoned. You take no pleasure in the length of your swing, and you take no pleasure in the length of your relationships. Slow down, Don. You don't have to *have* the assistants to enjoy them. Just *be* with them. Then, whatever happens, happens."

"Wow. I'm embarrassed by my shallowness."

"Don't be. Don't judge, just grow."

"Yeah, you're right. Do you think Rhiannon likes me at all?"

"Don, did you hear a word I just said?"

"No. I can't get Rhiannon out of my mind. I'm sorry, Doctor Von Hayes. I'm going to go play thirty-six holes of golf, maybe then I'll calm down. I'll try that slow backswing thing, maybe that'll help."

He got to the door, stopped, and turned.

"Has Morgana ever asked about me at all? Forget it. Sorry, Doctor Von Hayes, sorry I even mentioned it. You know what I'm going to do before I play golf? I'm going to swim out to Seal Rock. What is that, about a mile and a half? I'll do it three times. How old is Morgana, anyway? Twenty? Twenty-five?

"She's fifty."

"Get out of here!" he gasped.

"Her youth and beauty come from being totally centered," I said.

"Well, forget her. I don't date the older gals."

"Whatever you think is right, Don."

"You know what I think I'll do. I'm going to do the swimming, I'll do the golf, and then I'll run until it gets dark. Then I'll take a few cold showers, do push-ups till dawn, and then maybe, just maybe, I'll be able to get your assistants out of my head. I'll see you around, Doctor."

"Take it easy, Don."

As he left, George and Martha entered, arguing. I could tell they'd been drinking.

"No, Martha my darling. If we hadn't stopped in Solvang to get those stinky cheeses you so love to wallow in, we wouldn't be late," George said, slightly weaving.

"Wrong, Georgie-Porgie. You're the one who insisted that we stop at Cambria to buy some little leaded Civil War toy soldiers."

"They're for our son."

"Don't talk about our son. You're breaking the rule. Besides, our son's too old for toy soldiers. He's at Harvard."

"No, he's not, Martha. He graduated. Now, he's a golfer. A professional golfer who teaches at the Palm

Beach Golf and Racquet Club. Have you forgotten, Martha? Have you lost your mind? Have you gone insane?''

''For Christ's sake, Georgie, those soldiers weren't for him, they were for you. You think I can't see through that? That's so sad. When are you going to grow up?''

''You want me to grow up, Martha? Why don't you grow down. Like about fifty pounds down, mostly off your prodigious porcine hindquarters.''

''You must be George and Martha Meade,'' I interjected.

''Not for long,'' George snapped.

''Who are you?'' Martha snarled.

''I'm Doctor Bobby Von Hayes.''

''Oh, you are, are you? Look, George. A man. A real man.''

''Don't be taken in by her, Doctor Von Hayes. That way lies madness.''

''Do you two fight all the time?'' I asked.

''No. Sometimes I just resent her silently,'' George muttered.

''That's very kind of you, George,'' Martha seethed.

''My pleasure, darling.''

''I understand you two were put on probation by your country club. What happened?'' I asked.

''The truth is,'' Martha said, flirting, ''about a month ago, we had a real beauty of a brawl. We were playing in a best ball couples tournament at the Club, and George did what he always does. He started drinking too much and then he started criticizing my swing. A swing my Daddy taught to me when I was a little girl. You didn't know me then, George. I was happy."

"You weren't happy, Martha. You just thought you were."

"Thank you for denying my entire childhood, Georgie. Anyway, Doctor Von Hayes, Porgie Pig here wouldn't leave my swing alone. He can be such a contentious son-of-a-bitch. I got so mad I whipped my wedge at him. He grabbed a one-wood and chased me, past all of our friends, to a water hazard, where he pushed me in and tried to drown me."

"I didn't try to drown you, Martha."

"If Nicky hadn't pulled you off me, I would have drowned, and that's the truth."

"You wouldn't know the truth, Martha, if it came up and bit you on the rear. And you know why? Because you wouldn't feel it."

"Oh, that's so witty, George. It's too bad that the sad characters in your failed novel can't be so witty."

"Oh, another blow below the belt. But fortunately I didn't feel anything, because I've been dead from the waist down for years, thank you very much, Martha."

"Oh, screw you, George."

"No. Screw you, Martha."

"Look," I said. "I don't allow that kind of language or hostility at the Institute. Now, either you two control yourselves, or I'm going to have to ask you to leave."

"I apologize, Doctor Von Hayes. My wife and I tend to blur the distinction between private conversation and public display."

"Where was I?" Martha interrupted. "Oh, yes. The Club governing board put us on six months probation, with the provision that we could return only after receiving professional help. That's why we're here."

I found myself disliking this couple intensely. But, if I was to help them, I had to get past that. I had to remind myself that their anger for one another was probably passion that had been twisted by disappointment and hurt, ruining their love, their lives, and their game. My job was to find out what caused that hurt and start the healing process, so they could get back on course—and on the course. I suggested that we have a playing lesson, where I could observe, in more detail, the patterns of their behavior.

During the front nine they didn't talk to one another between shots. When George hooked a drive into the woods on the third, Martha wouldn't help him look for it. When Martha had a foot-long putt on the fifth green, George refused to give it to her. Furious, she missed it. Neither observed the common etiquette of waiting for the farthest player away to hit first. Often, they would both strike the ball at the same time, disrupting their mate's concentration. Generally, they showed no respect for one another's game.

It became so tense that I couldn't continue on to the back nine without breaking for lunch.

As we sat on the veranda, George and Martha explained they were on an all-liquid diet and ordered two double Tangueray gin martinis. By the time I'd finished my usual lovely jellied consommé they were well into their cups. In the distance, I could see Don Levy swimming out to Seal Rock, trying to drown his unsinkable lust.

"Are you married, Doctor Von Hayes?" Martha asked, running her hand up my thigh.

"No, I'm not, and what are you doing, Mrs. Meade?"

"What she tries to do with every man. Seduce and destroy."

"No, I'm not, Georgie. I'm just trying to find out if Doctor Von Hayes is gay."

"I'm not."

"I sensed that," she said, lightly stroking my fingers.

"Martha, will you stop this disgusting display," George sighed, nursing his martini.

Martha turned to George. "Doctor Von Hayes, do you know who would really like you? Our son."

"Martha. You're breaking the rule."

"But, George, you broke it already when we first got here. Remember? It's fair game now." She turned back to me. "Our son needs a father figure. Georgie-Porgie Puddin' and Pie has been such a failure in that area."

"Don't talk about our son, Martha. Don't make me do it."

"You wouldn't," she said.

"I would," he countered.

"You're not man enough," she taunted.

I realized I was witnessing a classic case of psychoneurotic gamesmanship which had been finely honed over many years and many rounds of golf and drinks. What was really going on here, I wondered?

George pulled himself up and swayed in front of me. "Excuse me, Doctor Von Hayes. I need to use the men's room before we begin the back nine."

"Oh, good. Take your time, George," Martha said, boozily.

George stumbled off the veranda.

Martha looked at me hungrily. "Why don't we leave George here and just you and me play the back nine, Doctor Von Hayes? You know, have a private lesson," she said, winking.

"I don't think that would be appropriate."

"Oh, sure it would, Bobby. Trust me. George is so bombed, he won't even notice we're gone. You know what's funny? Bobby's our son's name."

"No, it's not, Martha," George said. We turned to see him standing behind us. "Martha, I have some tragic news."

"What is it now, Georgie?"

"It's about our son."

"Don't do it, George."

"There's been an accident."

"God damn it, George. I'm warning you . . ."

"Apparently, he was giving a golf lesson and a stray ball hit him . . ."

"Stop it! Stop it, George!"

" . . . and killed him instantly. Our son is dead!"

"I'm so sorry," I said. "How can I help you?"

"Stay out of it!" Martha shrieked. She turned on George. "It wasn't a golf ball that killed him, George. It was you! You did it!" she sobbed.

"I had to, Martha. It was killing us."

"What's going on here?" I asked.

"Welcome to the first honest moment in our twenty-year marriage. We have no son, Doctor. We invented him."

"Goddamn it, George!" Martha moaned. All rage drained from her. She sobbed unconsolably. Through her tears, I could see Martha's broken heart.

"It's all right, Martha." George went to his wife and put his arms around her. "I can't write and you can't have children. It's all right. It's all right, Martha. We have no more illusions."

"Then, we have nothing, George," she sobbed. "Don't you see? Without our illusion we have nothing."

"Excuse me, Mrs. Meade," I said, "am I to understand you invented a child to keep your marriage together?"

"Yes," George answered. "When we married, I was going to be a great novelist and we were going to have children."

"Lots of children," Martha added. "But I couldn't have them."

"And I couldn't write."

"All of which explains your bitter disappointment with each other and your anger on the golf course. And yet, you've stayed together."

"The only thing that kept us together was our invented son, not any love we had for each other," Martha said. "Now that we don't have him, it's over. It's all over."

"I'm not so sure," I said quietly. "I believe there's

still a vestige of love between you. I can see it. You may not play golf well together, but at least you're still playing."

They exchanged a cautious look.

"I'm intuiting something here. Tell me about the first time you two played golf together."

"Oh, that was in college. Daddy set us up on a blind date because he thought George was a writer with promise. George called me and asked if, instead of going to the theater to see *Zoo Story*, I'd like to play a round of golf. I thought it was really corny, but I said yes, even though I hadn't played since I was a little girl."

"That's right," George added. "It was the longest, most wonderful round of golf I ever played in my life. We started in the early afternoon and finished by moonlight. We had so much to talk about that we forgot we were playing, and finally, around the seventeenth, we just lay down on the fairway and looked up at the stars."

"George, how did Martha make you feel that night, under the stars?"

"As if I could tell her everything, and she'd understand."

"How about you, Martha?" I asked.

"He was the first boy I was ever with who didn't talk about himself and how wonderful he was. He actually listened to me. Of course, then we started kissing and he wanted to make love, but I wouldn't let him."

"I knew that night I wanted to marry her." George hung his head. "And now it's over. It's all over."

"It might be, and then again, it might not. You see, George and Martha, once you've lost the illusion that you *thought* was keeping you together, you've actually created the opportunity to begin your relationship all over again. I'd like to try something. I'd like the two of you to play the back nine and, when you do, I want to see if you can treat each other as if you were playing golf together for the very first time, like you did that night you fell in love on the golf course."

"How do we do that, Doctor?" Martha asked.

"The secret to playing with your mate is to treat each other with respect and kindness, as if you'd just met. We should always try to play that way. Err on the side of kindness. George, if Martha hits a ball into the rough, help her find it. Martha, if George has a one-foot putt, give it to him. Be gracious, be loving. George, if something's wrong with your wife's swing, don't criticize her. Help her change. Be constructive. Criticism is a dead end. It does more to alienate golfing couples than anything else I know. George? Martha? Shall we give the back nine a try? I mean, who's afraid of a little golf?"

At first, George and Martha were like awkward teenagers, not knowing how to be with each other. They were so used to treating each other with hostility that every attempted gracious gesture confused them. They managed by establishing a formal civility, but there was no warmth. I was sure they'd never finish the nine.

But, as I've told you before, golf therapy is powerful stuff. By the fifteenth, their formal civility had given way to experimental flirtatiousness. By the eighteenth hole, the two of them were walking down the middle of the fairway, actually talking with one another. At one point, Martha tossed her head back and laughed girlishly.

George hit a remarkable eight-iron that hit and stuck one foot from the pin. As George reached for his putter, Martha took his hand and held it.

"It's good, George."

After the round, we sat on the veranda having iced teas while the sun set over the sea.

"This was wonderful today, Doctor Von Hayes, but I'm scared," Martha said.

"Of what?" I asked.

"I'm afraid we're going to get in the car and the fighting will start all over again."

"It's what we do best," George said quietly.

"Well, that's a real possibility. You're at a very fragile moment right now. You're both very vulnerable and open. It's easy to fall back into old patterns. As your ongoing therapy I want you to play golf together, every day, for the next six months. The key, as I told you before, is to play as if you were meeting and playing together for the first time. If you work at it, you just might make it."

They did. A year later, I got a letter from George saying that he and Martha were living in Bermuda and had adopted a son. George has gone back to his novel, which he insists is still dreadful. Martha, on the other hand, is convinced it's a work of seminal genius.

Oh, by the way, Don Levy has left the Institute and is now training full-time for the Iron Man Triathlon in Hawaii. He says it's the only way he can keep my assistants off his mind. Poor Don.

CASE # 8:

How to Hit a Hole in One: Carlos Says Goodbye

Everyone wants to hit a hole in one. I've hit thousands and, believe me, it's no big deal. The key is not to *try* to hit a hole in one. The key is to allow a hole in one to happen to you. Golfers in the Western world strive for results, at the expense of process. We care more about obtaining low scores, low handicaps, winning a bet, or winning the club championship than we do about playing the game, finding out who we are, and using that knowledge to better ourselves and our game. The irony is, if we played the game as a self-integrating experience, we wouldn't care about holes in one. And, of course, the less we cared, the more we'd make.

The perfect example of this is Carlos, my golf ranger, who hit a hole in one on his first and only swing.

I was asleep in my chambers, dreaming that I was conducting a symphony orchestra made up of all the world's great golfers and psychologists. Freud was my first violinist, Hogan played the oboe, Jung the clarinet, and Bobby Jones was on the kettle drum. Freud was angry at Jung, because he thought Jung's clarinet was drowning out his violin. I pointed out to Freud that he wasn't the conductor, I was. And if he continued to behave that way I'd replace him with Fritz Perls. Freud sheepishly sat down. I raised my baton and, on my signal, this hundred-piece orchestra of great golfers and psychologists harmoniously began Beethoven's Sixth Symphony.

I was awakened by the sound of pebbles striking my French window. "Hey, fella! Fella!" a voice cried from below.

I climbed out of bed, threw open the French windows, and saw Carlos, standing below.

"I've got to talk to you!" Carlos called up to me.

"Carlos, can't it wait till the morning?"

"No. I'm leaving tonight."

"I'll be right down."

I dressed quickly and joined Carlos on the veranda. The moon was full and bright and a gentle salt sea breeze cooled the late night air.

"I'm not very good at saying goodbye, Doctor."

"Why are you going?" I asked.

Carlos attempts a hole in one.

"A voice inside me says 'go.' "

"Then you should listen, Carlos."

"I always have. Problem is that voice has gotten me into a lot of trouble."

"I suspect it's gotten you *out* of a lot of trouble, too."

"Yeah, it has," Carlos said sadly.

"Where are you going?"

"Back to Tahiti. I'm going to sell the island. It's a tourist trap now. Too many fat Americans like me over there."

"What are you going to do?"

"I've been offered six million dollars to play Freddy's grandfather in *Nightmare on Elm Street, Part whatever-the-hell-it-is.* I'll probably do it. I thought I could go on playing the Carlos role forever, but I can't. I've never been able to play just one part."

"That's because you have so many selves. That's why you're our greatest actor."

"I hate acting."

"You shouldn't. Acting's been a good friend to you. It's allowed those selves to come alive, bringing pleasure and insight to millions of people."

"I'm tired of serving all those selves and all those voices. I want to be one, whole, simple person."

"I hear that."

"That's why playing Carlos was so great. He could go out in the "Bounty" and collect floating golf balls, go home, light a lantern, listen to the wind, and go to sleep—dreamlessly. Now this voice inside me says 'go.' I don't want to go. I love it here. I love what you're doing here, and I really thought I could be Carlos forever." He sighed, exhausted. "I'm too old to change."

"Let's try something. Let me get a club and a ball and let's continue this conversation out on the fourth tee. I mean, if you're not in a rush to leave?"

"I guess I can wait for a while."

We went into my study. From over the mantelpiece I took my most prized club, a George Sayer one-wood. George himself had hand-forged it in Scotland in the early forties. It was a remarkable club, four inches longer than a normal one. He gave it to me when he had become too old to wield it. The one-wood had become my Excalibur. My Sword in the Stone.

I took two Penfold golf balls that I'd used to win the Nepal Open and we wandered out through the cypress trees to the fourth tee. Of all the holes that I'd designed on this course, I was the proudest of this one. It's not that it was particularly long—it's only three hundred and ninety yards—but the elevated tee shot had to carry two hundred and twenty yards over the bay to a narrow fairway that doglegged left down to the green, which was nestled in the rocks along the shore. When I'm feeling particularly strong, and there's a downwind, I will sometimes try to cut the dogleg by going directly to the hole.

"Have you ever had a hole in one?" I asked Carlos.

"I've never played golf."

"Never?"

"I've never even swung a club."

"Perfect. Welcome to your first and last lesson: how

to hit a hole in one. I have a theory. I believe that if you're integrated and living the life you're meant to lead, you can get a hole in one. No matter the distance of the hole, no matter if it's day or night, no matter if you've never even swung a golf club. Shall we test my theory?''

"All right."

"There are two ways to approach this hole. The safe, conservative way, which is to hit over the water to the fairway; or our way, which is to hit over the cypress trees and go directly to the cup."

"I love it. I've spent my whole life trying shots like that," Carlos said, metaphorically.

"Good." I teed the ball up and, just to make things interesting, closed my eyes. I could tell by the way the club head struck the ball that I had hit a perfect draw. Long and true.

"I never saw it," Carlos said.

"Neither did I, but it felt good. You're up."

"What do I do?"

"Stick the tee in the ground, put the ball on the tee, and hit it."

"You keep things simple, don't you, Doctor?

"With complicated spirits like you, I do."

He laughed, approached the ball, and swung. The club face's impact cracked like a gunshot, but his ball went directly left, toward the open sea.

"Oh, look at that!" he said derisively. "What an awful shot."

"Have a little faith."

With this, his ball carved a long banana arc to the right, across the full moon, and over the trees.

"God damn!" he said.

"Please don't swear, and let's go find our balls."

"Hey, Doctor, I don't know about yours, but mine is long gone. We'll never find it."

We walked the three hundred and ninety-five yards in silence, lost in our thoughts. I knew our shots had gone in. I strolled confidently onto the green and looked into the hole. The cup was empty.

"Well?" Carlos said, catching up to me.

"It's empty," I said, shocked.

"Did you really think they'd be in there?"

"Yes. Something's wrong."

"Yeah. It's you and me. We're both crazy."

"No, that's not it. It's something else," I said, putting the flag back into the hole.

We started to walk off when the sound of the flag fluttering turned me around. I saw the flag in the moonlight, the number "5" waving at me. I started running.

"Where are you going?" Carlos called after me.

"We're on the wrong green! We lost our way in the dark! The fourth is over here!"

We ran a hundred yards to the left and onto the fourth green.

"Go ahead, Carlos. Take a look."

He walked up to the hole, looked down, and turned back to me, beaming like a child.

"They're here."

"I knew it."

He knelt down, took the two Penfolds out of the cup, and showed them to me. He stayed on his knees for a long time, then laughed so hard, tears ran down his cheeks.

"I get it!" he shouted to the stars. "I understand the hole in one!"

He jumped up, clicked his heels, and danced a tarantella around the green. "I get it! I get it! Whoopee! Yeah!" he howled to the moon. "I *am* the hole in one! I *am* the hole in one!"

"Exactly!" I said.

"All those different voices in me, are me! I've spent my whole life trying to simplify myself, to become just one voice, but that's wrong, isn't it? I am *all* those voices. That's what the hole in one tells me."

"That's right," I said, "and the key is to discern which voice to listen to, and when."

"Right," he said. "I thought I could just be Carlos, but I can't."

"Well, part of you is Carlos, and the rest of you is so much more."

"I know that now." He fell silent. "What I don't know is what to do now."

"Do what you've always done. Act."

"I'm sick of acting. It's phony and embarrassing."

"No, it isn't. It's the one vehicle that allows you to give expression to all of your selves. All of your voices. You are Stanley Kowalski, you are Don Corleone, you are the Wild One."

"But I quit acting. I can't go back."

"You've got to. We need you. Don't you see? All those voices in you are our voices, too. Don't you understand? We need you to speak for us. Come back, Marlon. Come back."

He looked at me, a smile briefly lighting his face, as a cloud passed over the moon.

"Keep that Penfold to remind you of who you are."

We hugged farewell, and I watched this great and lonely bear disappear among the redwoods. I stood alone, under the heavens, and felt the loss of a friend, leaving.

Epilogue

The Healing Tour

Now that you've read the eight cases and understand what golf therapy is all about, some of you may be starting to deify me. Golfers do that to me all the time. After all, I am the only golf therapist in the world, and maybe the universe, who knows? But don't deify me. Not only is it dangerous, it means you've missed the main point of golf therapy. *You are your own golf therapist.* I'm not a teacher, I'm not a guide, I'm not a saint. I'm simply a reminder of who you are.

For those of you who want to delve deeper into the mysteries of golf therapy, come visit me at my Institute in Big Sur, California. My Tantric assistants and I would love to see you.

In fact, if you have the time, why don't you join us on my annual golf pilgrimage, or what I like to call the World Healing Tour. At the beginning of every Spring Equinox, we leave California and travel east, to Scotland, where we play the Old Course at St. Andrews. We then layover in Paris, where we visit the museums, play a round or two at the Royal Greens of Versailles, stroll along the Champs-Elysees, and breathe in its spring blossom scents. But mostly we just goof off and try to pick up girls.

Next, it's off to Switzerland, where we visit the homes of Carl Jung and Herman Hesse and play three old Alpine courses, where the only groundskeepers are sheep. Then it's on to ancient Rome. More girls, more museums, more golf. Then to Nepal, where we stay at the Minya Konka monastery and meditate with my guru Radha, a seven-foot tall, blonde, Nepalese golfing goddess. Each morning at dawn we rise and play the course, where every hole is a different stop on life's journey. After a round of golf there, believe me, you and your game will never be the same.

Then we begin our journey home, stopping in Tahiti, where we stay for a couple of weeks—or for however long it takes to unwind—at "Carlos's" island. At last, we take a slow boat home, where every evening at sunset we hit shots off the stern into our wake.

Won't you join us?